Computer Science Principles

The Foundational Concepts of Computer Science

Kevin Hare

with a foreword by Pindar Van Arman

YELLOW DART PUBLISHING

4th Edition

All inquiries should be addressed to:
Yellow Dart Publishing
info@apcompsciprinciples.com

Microsoft product screenshots used with permission from Microsoft

Adobe product screenshots reprinted with permission from Adobe
Systems Incorporated.

Adobe® and Adobe® Photoshop are either registered trademarks or
trademarks of Adobe Systems Incorporated in the United States
and/or other countries.

Google and the Google logo are registered trademarks of Google Inc.,
used with permission

ISBN:
Paperback: 978-1-7345549-3-9
Hardcover: 978-1-7345549-4-6
eBook: 978-1-7345549-5-3

To Parker and Quinn,

49204c6f766520796f7521

-K.H.

Computer Science Principles

5 - Protecting Data: Heuristics, Security, and Encryption

6 - The Internet

Software Alternatives

This book discusses a wide variety of concepts but also explores a few specific pieces of software. These programs may require a large one-time payment or—more commonly today—a monthly fee. Other software, like many smartphone apps, earn revenue from an advertising-based model. Many applications discussed in this book offer a free-trial period that you can use to try out a product before purchasing it.

Free and open-source software (FOSS, discussed in unit 9) allows users and developers the freedom to share and improve upon software. FOSS allows users to use software without charge, it also allows them to access and modify the source code. The following FOSS applications can be used to accomplish similar tasks and to open the same file types as Excel, Photoshop, or Dreamweaver.

LibreOffice is similar to the Microsoft Office suite and includes applications for word processing, spreadsheets, slideshows, databases and more. It can be used in place of Excel in unit 4. Created from OpenOffice in 2010, it can be found at https://www.libreoffice.org/

GIMP (GNU Image Manipulation Program) can be used as an alternative to Photoshop (discussed in unit 2.5). This free and open-source software is used to manipulate raster images. More information can be found at https://www.gimp.org/

Photopea, an ad-supported web-based image editor, has a very similar look, feel, and workflow to Photoshop, including the ability to edit .PSD files. Since nothing needs to be downloaded, Photopea makes a great substitute for Photoshop, especially for Chrome Book users. Photopea can be found at https://photopea.com

Brackets is a free and open-source text editor created by Adobe. It is an excellent free solution for web development and can serve as an alternative to expensive website building software. Although any text editor and web browser can be used to create web pages, Brackets has a variety of tools to help with the workflow. It can be downloaded at http://brackets.io/

Numerous other applications, both free and paid, can perform similar tasks, and more are being created and updated every day. As you explore and dive deeper into specific topics, research and explore the software that best fits your needs.

0 - Foreword

I envy readers of this computer science book. It's not like the book I started out with. That book was filled with exercises that resembled math problems. Algorithms were described along with demonstrations of the most efficient way to use them. We were then challenged to solve these problems in the most efficient way possible. It's not that these exercises weren't fun, but they were very rigid and usually had a single correct answer. This put creative types like me at a disadvantage. I wanted to experiment with software and try different approaches, even if they were not the best approaches. The book I remember was not designed for that. It emphasized efficiency over creativity.

But this book is different. Computer science is a creative field, and this book's approach celebrates this creativity. This book will put you well on your way to understanding how to use modern software applications, what makes them work, and how you can improve on them to write your own applications.

As an artist, I think this creative approach is the most interesting way to tackle any problem.

My art is a little unusual. I design creative algorithms then have several custom robots use these algorithms to create paintings, one brushstroke at a time. These AI generated paintings are a record of both how far I have come in the discipline of computational creativity, and how far artificial intelligence in general has developed.

My most recent painting robot project is called CloudPainter, and it can paint some wonderful paintings. I named it CloudPainter not because every new computer-related thing needs to have the word "cloud" in it, but because I want my latest robots to be able to look into the clouds and be inspired by them to create their artwork. We humans might notice that a cloud resembles a dragon and use that as inspiration to let our imaginations run wild. I wanted my robots to be able to do the exact same thing. I wanted them to imagine the images they painted.

We have had some success toward that goal. While my earliest robots were relatively simple machines that dipped a brush in paint and dragged the brush around a canvas, my most recent robots use dozens of artificial intelligence algorithms, a handful of deep-learning neural networks, and continuous feedback loops to paint with increasing creative autonomy.

Exactly how far has their creativity come?

Famed *New York* magazine art critic Jerry Saltz recently reviewed one of my robotic paintings. Speaking of the Portrait of Elle Reeve, he began it "doesn't look like this was made by a computer." He then paused and continued, "That doesn't make it any good." It sounds like a bad review, but I loved it. A couple years ago, no one even considered our paintings to be art. Now people at least think they're bad art. That's progress!

To make a portrait that didn't look like a computer made it, my robots used all their creative abilities to re-imagine Elle Reeve's face in an abstract impressionist style then painted it based on strokes modeled from a famous Picasso.

Jerry Saltz' admission that this painting could have been done by a human hand was a major milestone in my artistic career. As I mentioned, few have even acknowledged my art as art. Some looked at my painting robots and called them over-engineered printers. Other naysayers complained that our paintings were little more than images run through the equivalent of a Photoshop filter.

Beyond the robots and their paintings, people often took offense at the very idea of what I was trying to do, which was to create artistic robots. For many it was a grotesque attempt to mimic the very essence of what makes us human. My attempts threatened and worried people. I remember one exhibition where an artist pulled me over and said "I don't know whether to be impressed or disgusted with your work."

Over the years, however, there also have been many who understood exactly what I was trying to accomplish. The author of this book, Kevin Hare, was one of them. We first met while teaching in Washington, DC. Kevin was a computer science teacher. I taught art. My friendship with Kevin was unexpected. Our classrooms were on opposite sides of campus, and one would think that there would be little overlap in our curriculum. As we got to know each other, however, it quickly became apparent that we were on similar wavelengths. We both realized the creative power of software. We had many conversations where we discussed the similarities between our creative processes. Both of us realized just how similar writing code was to making art.

As I read this book, I was reminded of many things he shared with me about the creative aspects of computer design. You will find it in his style as well as in the exercises he provides. This book does not just ask you to complete a task for the sake of completing it. It challenges you to have fun with the code to do things that you are interested in.

His concern for keeping your interest can even be seen in the order in which he covers the material. The book begins by introducing the basics, as would be expected, but then it does something unusual. The second unit goes right into the creative side of software by exploring photo editing. As an artist, this made perfect sense to me. It even mirrored my own journey into computer science. The first programs I used were photo editing tools like Photoshop. As I needed these tools to do more than they were capable of, I found myself writing my own. This got me started in computer science and eventually led to my AI robots.

The truly fun part of computer science is learning how to use code to be better at the things you love. Kevin Hare understands this perfectly and goes out of his way to teach you things that have interesting practical applications.

At its core, software is a tool that helps us do things much more efficiently. Simple programs like word processors let us write more words per minute. Spreadsheets let us do complex accounting and analysis. More complex programs like Photoshop and Garage Band help us make art and compose music. Those of us who take the time to understand and master these tools have a great advantage over those who do not.

Do you like playing an instrument? Unit seven will help you make a website for your band. Like making art, like I do? Creative applications are discussed in multiple units, beginning with unit two. Want to make billions of dollars creating the hot new crypto-currency? Look no further than unit five's discussion of cryptography.

Regardless of your interest, this book will get you started on the path to writing software that helps you excel. Making yourself better at whatever you want to be better at has never been easier.

Pindar Van Arman
Creator, *CloudPainter*
www.cloudpainter.com

1 - Hardware, Software, Number Systems, and Boolean Expressions

"It's hardware that makes a machine fast. It's software that makes a fast machine slow."

- Craig Bruce

Introduction

If you have ever turned on a phone or surfed the Internet then you have used a computer and should have a basic understanding of what happens when you click the mouse or touch the screen—and how fast it happens! A **computer** is an electronic device that processes data according to a set of instructions or commands, known as a program. Before creating spreadsheets, manipulating images, understanding the Internet, making websites, encrypting data, or learning how to code, it is important to understand the basics of every computer. All computers—desktops, laptops, tablets, and smartphones—convert data into ones and zeros and have the same basic components: software and hardware. In this unit, we'll define some of computing's most basic terms and explore how computers work at the most elemental level.

Software

At the lowest level, computer **software** is just a series of ones and zeros. It cannot be touched physically and is usually stored on the computer's hard drive. We can consider software as belonging in two general categories: the operating system and the applications.

The **operating system** (OS) includes the desktop, start menu, icons, file manager, and common services shared by other programs. It manages hardware and software resources and provides the visual (graphical or text-based) representation of the computer. Again, at its most basic level, the software is just a series of ones and zeros—usually billions of them at any one time—that cannot usually be understood by a human, so the operating system helps make these ones and zeros easy to read and understand. Some popular operating systems include Windows 10, MacOS Catalina, and GNU/Linux.

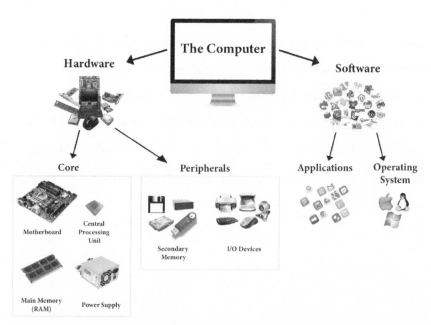

Pretty much everything else on your computer, except for saved files, are **applications,** including word processors, photo editing software, web browsers, games, and music players. A few popular applications include Microsoft Office, Adobe Photoshop, Apple Music, Google Chrome, and Fortnite.

Hardware

The physical parts of the computer are known as **hardware**. These devices—such as the monitor, keyboard, speakers, wires, chips, cables, plugs, disks, printers, mice, and many other items—can be touched. There are two categories of hardware: the **core** and the **peripherals**. The core is made up of the motherboard, the central processing unit (CPU), the main memory, and the power supply. Peripherals consist of the input and output (I/O) devices and the secondary memory.

Everything that happens on a computer goes through the core. Together, the core components—motherboard, CPU, main memory, and power supply—do all the heavy lifting in the computer.

Also called a logic board, a **motherboard** is the standardized printed circuit board that connects the CPU, main memory, and peripherals to each other. Since many different manufacturers make parts for computers, there are a handful of standard form factors to make sure circuits and hardware fit together properly. Most motherboards also contain a small integrated chip and firmware, which stores the **BIOS**—or *basic input/output system*—as a way to communicate with the computer (especially before an operating system exists). The **POST** (or power-on self-test) process is also found in this firmware. POST runs basic checks to make sure all core components and peripherals are powering on correctly, usually verified by a chime or series of lights on the motherboard.

The **Central Processing Unit (CPU)** carries out every command or process on the computer. It can be described as the brain of the computer, and it is extremely fast, with a speed that is usually measured in gigahertz—billions of processes per second. By the time information gets to the CPU, it is broken down to ones and zeros. One of the reasons it can process so many commands is because it only needs to recognize these two numbers.

The **main memory** temporarily stores information while it is being sent to the CPU. It also helps break down information to something the CPU can easily understand. Main memory can be thought of as the core's "bouncer." Everything that happens goes through the main memory first. The main memory is often referred to as **RAM**, or **random-access memory**. In other words, information can be retrieved from or written to any location in the memory. The computer does not have to go through everything stored in the memory to get to the information at the very end. Think about old cassette tapes. To get to the next song, the current song needs to be either played all the way through or fast forwarded through. This kind of memory is called **sequential memory**. RAM is more like a CD. To get the next song, just hit next.

Remember, the main memory temporarily holds information while the CPU processes it. As a result, the more RAM a computer has, the less often it needs to retrieve information and—all other things being equal—the faster it can run programs and the more programs it can run simultaneously.

Just like the power adapter on other electronic devices, a computer's **power supply** converts AC power from the electrical grid to the lower voltage DC power that is needed to power the computer's components. Most power supplies contain a fan to keep them cool and a switch to change between different voltages.

Nearly everything else in the computer is called a **peripheral**, which means it operates at the outside edge of the computer. A user interacts with a computer through peripherals—not the CPU or main memory. Peripherals include the secondary memory, all input and output devices, video or graphics cards, and more.

Secondary memory is all memory accessed by the computer, except the main memory. It is used for long-term storage and is physically changed whenever files are saved or deleted. This change makes secondary memory slower than the main memory—although it is still very fast. Secondary memory is much larger than the main memory, and changes are usually only made when a user alters the information stored there, for instance when saving or deleting a file. Common secondary memory devices include hard drives, floppy disks, CD-ROMs, USB storage devices, and flash drives. These peripherals store the software (both OS and applications) that the main memory will access.

A user interacts with a computer using **input and output (I/O) devices**. Without them, computers would not be very useful. Input devices allow users to send instructions or data to a computer. Keyboards and mice are the most common input devices. They tell the computer when something is typed or clicked. Other input devices include joysticks, microphones, and scanners. Output devices take something from the computer and send it to the user. Monitors and printers are the most common output devices. Others include speakers and virtual reality goggles. Some devices provide both input and output. A touchscreen, for example, takes input when touched and also displays output as a monitor.

Main memory is usually volatile while secondary memory tends to be non-volatile. The distinction here has to do with the stored information and the power supply. In the case of **volatile** memory, information is lost when the power is turned off whereas with **non-volatile** memory, the information remains. So when you shut down your computer, the main memory is wiped clean, but—thankfully—the secondary memory will remain as is!

Remember that a computer —at its lowest level—only reads zeros and ones. You can think of a computer like a light switch: it is either on or off. When it comes to RAM, a computer can just mark the "switch" on or off, but floppy disks and CD-ROMs work a little differently. Floppy disks are magnetic, and CDs and DVDs use light. A CD has a smooth surface with pits. The smooth parts represent zeros, and the pits stand for ones. In the case of CD-Rs and CD-RWs, the surface becomes reflective when heated to one temperature and non-reflective when heated to another.

Computing Systems

There are several different models that computers can use to solve problems. **Sequential computing** is a model in which operations are performed in order, one at a time. This means that the total time it takes to complete a sequential solution is the sum of all of its steps. While this approach can be effective for certain types of problems, it can be limiting when it comes to solving more complex issues.

Parallel computing, on the other hand, breaks a program into multiple smaller sequential computing operations, some of which are performed simultaneously. This allows for solutions to be completed more quickly than with sequential computing, but there is still a limit to how much it can scale. The efficiency of a parallel computing solution is still limited by the sequential portion, which means that at some point, adding parallel portions will no longer meaningfully increase efficiency.

Distributed computing is a model that involves using multiple devices to run a program. This approach allows for problems to be solved that would be too time-consuming or require too much storage to be solved on a single computer. With distributed computing, much larger problems can be solved more quickly than with a single computer.

Cloud computing is a type of distributed computing that has become increasingly popular in recent years. It involves using a network of remote servers to store, manage, and process data. Cloud computing allows for greater flexibility and scalability, as resources can be quickly and easily scaled up or down as needed. Additionally, cloud computing can be more cost-effective than traditional computing models, as users only pay for the resources they use. Overall, these models of computing have opened up exciting new possibilities for solving complex problems, handling large amounts of data, and have made collaboration more accessible.

Number Systems

In everyday use, we use a numeral system that uses numerals from zero to nine. So, for every number there are ten different options in each place. As in decagon or decathlon, the prefix *dec-* means ten, so it makes sense that the name of our numeral system starts with *dec-*. The numeral system we ordinarily use is called base-ten, or *deci*mal, and it uses ten numerals ranging from zero to nine, which are also called **digits**. In base-two, or **binary,** there are only two numerals used: zero and one. As in the words bicycle, bifocal, or bipartisan, the prefix *bi-* means two, so each numeral in binary is called a *bit*, which is the smallest unit of information that a computer can process: zero or one, off or on. These bits are so small that it is more practical to group them into bunches of eight, otherwise known as **bytes**.

Each address in memory contains one byte of information, but all except the most rudimentary units of information are larger than one byte, so storing them requires multiple bytes. With today's computers, a byte is an exceedingly small amount of memory, so instead of talking about them in the millions or billions, we use the larger units below. Since the computer only processes zeros and ones, everything is measured in base-two, so one byte is two to the zeroth power, or one. The next unit is the kilobyte, which is two to the tenth power, or 1,024. Notice that a kilobyte contains more than one-thousand bytes, the usual meaning of the prefix *kilo*. A megabyte is 2^{20}, a gigabyte 2^{30}, and a terabyte 2^{40}.

Unit	# of bytes	# of bytes	~bytes
byte	2^0	1	One
kilobyte	2^{10}	1,024	One-thousand
megabyte	2^{20}	1,048,576	One-million
gigabyte	2^{30}	1,073,741,824	One-billion
terabyte	2^{40}	1,099,511,627,776	One-trillion

Sometimes when companies release hardware, such as hard drives or smartphones, they will consider a megabyte as one-million bytes instead of 2^{20} bytes or a gigabyte as one-billion bytes instead of 2^{30} bytes. If an mp3 player is advertised as having a capacity of twenty gigabytes, the company will put only twenty-billion bytes of memory in it, when twenty gigabytes actually means approximately 21.475 billion bytes. In this case, the customer has been shorted and really bought fewer than 19 GB of storage when they were expecting a full 20 GB.

Understanding the base-ten, or decimal, system will make understanding the base-two, or binary, system easier. Binary works in the same exact way as decimal, except that the digits range from zero to one. Therefore, instead of using powers of ten, binary uses powers of two. For example, the first digit is multiplied by 2^0, not 10^0, the second digit is multiplied by 2^1, not 10^1, and so forth. From right to left, the places in the decimal system go 1, 10, 100, 1000... (that is: 10^0, 10^1, 10^2, 10^3...). In binary, they go 1, 2, 4, 8, 16, 32, 64... (that is: 2^0, 2^1, 2^2, 2^3, 2^4, 2^5, 2^6...). Here is an example of a binary number: 1101 0010.

Converting Binary → Decimal

To convert from binary to decimal, simply add the values in binary that are "on" (1 represents on and 0 represents off).

```
1 0 0 1 = 8 + 1 = 9
8 4 2 1

1 1 1 1 = 8 + 4 + 2 + 1 = 15
8 4 2 1

  0   1   0   1  1  1  0  0 = 64 + 16 + 8 + 4 = 92
128 64 32 16 8 4 2 1
```

Converting Decimal → Binary

To convert decimal to binary, simply figure out (from left to right) if the binary value needs to be "on" (or a 1). If turning the value on does not make the sum of the number exceed the number, then it should be a 1 (otherwise it is a 0).

```
23 → 1 0 1 1 1 → 16 is on since it is less than 23,
     16 8 4 2 1    8 is off since 16 + 8 is greater than 23

46 → 1 0 1 1 1 0 → 32 is on since it is less than 46,
     32 16 8 4 2 1   16 is off since 32 + 16 is greater than 46

101 → 1 1 0 0 1 0 1 → 64 is on since it is less than 101,
      64 32 16 8 4 2 1   32 is on since 64+32 is less than 101
```

Hexadecimal (also known as **base 16**) is a common number system used in computer science. Since there are only ten digits (0-9), the first six letters are used to represent the remaining six characters (a-f). Each character in hexadecimal represents four bits (or a half of a byte). To represent a full byte, two hexadecimal characters are used. These range from **00** (representing 0) to **ff** (representing 255). The chart on the following page shows what each hexadecimal digit represents:

Decimal	Hexadecimal	Binary
0	0	0000 0000
1	1	0000 0001
2	2	0000 0010
3	3	0000 0011
4	4	0000 0100
5	5	0000 0101
6	6	0000 0110
7	7	0000 0111
8	8	0000 1000

9	9	0000 1001
10	a	0000 1010
11	b	0000 1011
12	c	0000 1100
13	d	0000 1101
14	e	0000 1110
15	f	0000 1111

When a hexadecimal number is larger than a **nybble** (or half of a byte), the left-most hex digit is worth more, as with any other base. In the decimal number 123, the 3 is worth 3 since it is in the ones place, but the 1 is worth 100 since it is in the hundreds place.

Converting Hexadecimal → Binary

To convert a hexadecimal number into binary, look at each nybble individually:

```
d3b → d = 1101, 3 = 0011, b = 1011 → 1101 0011 1011

40f → 4 = 0100, 0 = 0000, f = 1111 → 0100 0000 1111
```

To convert these to decimal, just follow the steps to convert binary to decimal from earlier in this unit.

Converting Binary → Hexadecimal

To convert from binary to hexadecimal, just follow the reverse of above:

```
1001 1100 0001 → 1001 = 9, 1100 = c, 0001 = 1 → 9c1

0110 0011 1110 → 0110 = 6, 0011 = 3, 1110 = e → 63e
```

We have ten fingers, so it makes sense that our society uses base-ten. It makes early counting simple. Since all of us have been using base-ten since preschool, we find it easy to work with. Some have argued, however, that **base-eight** or **octal** would be the easiest system to use, especially in computing. Since base-ten uses numerals 0–9, base-eight uses 0–7 (there is no 8 or 9). These numerals could be eight symbols or emojis, as long as everyone agreed on a standard. For this example, let's stick with 0–7. The ones place (10^0) would still be the ones place (8^0), but the tens place (10^1) would be the eights place (8^1). Every place after that would increase by a power of eight instead of by a power of ten (or a power of two in the case of binary and a power of sixteen in the case of hexadecimal).

Converting Octal → Decimal

Converting base-eight is just like converting binary, but instead of the places doubling, they increase by a power of eight:

```
174 → 1 7 4  → 1*64 + 7*8 + 4*1 = 64 + 56 + 4 = 124
       64 8 1
520 → 5 2 0  → 5*64 + 2*8 + 0*1 = 320 + 16 + 0 = 336
       64 8 1
```

ASCII and Character Encoding

ASCII stands for American Standard Code for Information Interchange. Computers can only understand numbers, so letters and symbols must be converted into numbers. This standard provides an agreed-upon protocol to encode other characters as numbers. This includes lowercase letters, uppercase letters, symbols, spaces, tabs, delete, backspace, and more. The first 32 characters (0-31) were used for teletype machines and are now considered obsolete. Most modern character encoding systems, like Unicode, are based on ASCII but allow for the encoding of many more characters, including other alphabets and emojis.

Boolean Logic

Boolean algebra or **Boolean logic** is a branch of algebra where variables can only have two values: true or false. Introduced in the mid-1800s by George Boole and used in a variety of applications, Boolean logic has become prevalent in digital electronics and programming.

There are three basic operations in Boolean logic: AND, OR, and NOT, also known as conjunction, disjunction, and negation respectively. There are several ways to represent each of these basic operations, which are also known as gates, including using the words AND, OR, and NOT. AND operations can also be represented with a conjunction symbol ($\land$), an ampersand (&), or several other methods including, as we will see in the programming unit, two ampersands (&&). OR operations can use the disjunction symbol ($\lor$), a pipe (|), an addition symbol (+), or a double pipe (||). NOT operations can use the negation symbol ($\neg$), a tilde ($\sim$), a caret ($\land$), an exclamation mark (!), or a horizontal bar above other expressions. For the examples in this unit, we will use $\land$, $\lor$, and $\neg$.

We will also use a fourth operation, *exclusive or*, that is a combination of other basic operations. Symbolized as XOR, this operation can also be represented by a plus sign inside a circle ($\oplus$).

Operation	Symbol
AND	∧
OR	∨
NOT	¬
XOR	⊕

AND

When an expression uses an AND operation, then both sides of the expression must be true in order for the entire expression to evaluate to true. The expression A ∧ B is only true if both A *and* B are true. Consider the eligibility requirements for President of the United States. Two requirements are that you must be at least 35-years old AND you must be a natural born citizen. If you are younger than 35, you may not serve as president even if you are a natural born citizen. Likewise, if you are 35 or older but are not a natural born citizen, you cannot be president. Both conditions must be true for the expression to be true.

OR

When the OR operation is used between two expressions, then only one thing has to be true for the entire expression to evaluate to true. If both things are true then the expression satisfies this requirement that at least one thing be true, so it evaluates to true. The only way an expression containing only OR operations can evaluate to false is if all included statements are false. Therefore, in the expression A ∨ B, if A is true the entire expression is true regardless of what B is. It is also true if B is true, regardless of A's truth or falsity. Think about the requirements to see an R-rated movie: You must be 17-years old OR be accompanied by someone who is 21-years old or older. If you are accompanied by a 21+ year old, your age doesn't matter. If you are 17+, it doesn't matter whether or not you are accompanied by someone over the age of 21.

NOT

The NOT operation simply reverses the associated expression. If the expression evaluates to true, it becomes false and if it is false, it becomes true. ¬A evaluates to false if A is true and vice versa. To evaluate ¬ (A ∧ B), first follow the order of operations and evaluate the parenthesis first. So if—and only if—A and B are both false then A ∧ B would be false. The entire expression would then be ¬ false, and something that is NOT false is true.

XOR

As we will see below, in actual logic gates, an *exclusive or* operator is made up of AND and OR gates. But the idea behind them is as simple as basic logic operations. If two expressions are separated by an XOR operator then *exactly one* of those things must be true. If neither or both are true then the whole expression is false. In A ⊕ B, either A needs to be true and B needs to be false *or* B needs to be true and A needs to be false for the expression to be true. Think about having to choose between taking the bus or driving to school. You cannot do both and if you do neither, you will miss computer science class! To be at school, you must choose exactly one way to get there. If an expression contains multiple XOR operators then it will be true when it contains an odd number of true statements. To see this in action, try drawing the gates and filling out a truth table with three, four, five, or more XOR gates, as described in the next section.

Logic Gates

A **logic gate** is a physical device that can carry out logical operations by taking one or more Boolean values as input and producing one Boolean value as output. When talking about computers, these two Boolean values are 0 and 1. In electronic circuits, a 0 represents no current running through the wire and 1 represents current running through the wire.

The physical process of creating the basic gates and the XOR gate is outside the scope of this book, but by adding a level of **abstraction—** reducing information and detail to facilitate focus on relevant concepts—these gates can be represented with the following symbols:

AND   OR   NOT   XOR

The inputs are usually represented with A, B, C, D, etc. while the final result is represented with an R. Notice that NOT gates only take one input.

XOR gates are not basic gates. Rather, they can be created by combining the basic gates AND, OR, and NOT. There are several ways to construct XOR gates, one of which is pictured below. These details can be abstracted out and the XOR symbol used instead.

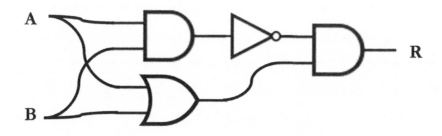

Truth Tables

When evaluating Boolean expressions, it is helpful to write out all possible outcomes in a table where each column represents a variable or expression being evaluated. This **truth table** will show possible values for inputs and a true or false value for the overall expression's result.

Examples

A NOT gate and truth table using false and true and one input:

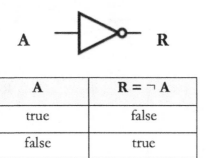

A	R = ¬ A
true	false
false	true

An AND gate and truth table using false and true with two inputs:

A	B	R = A ∧ B
false	false	false
false	true	false
true	false	false
true	true	true

An XOR gate and truth table using 0's and 1's with two inputs:

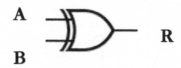

A	B	R = A ⊕ B
0	0	0
0	1	1
1	0	1
1	1	0

A more complicated circuit with three inputs and multiple gates:

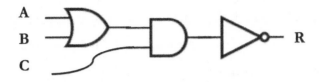

A	B	C	R = ¬ ((A ∨ B) ∧ C)
0	0	0	1
1	0	0	1
0	1	0	1
1	1	0	1
0	0	1	1
1	0	1	0
0	1	1	0
1	1	1	0

Summary

As we've explored in this unit, a computer is a machine, and at its most basic level, it is hardware—a physical thing that you can touch. On its own, hardware isn't useful as much more than a paperweight, but once software—the operating system, programs, and files—are added, it's a different story. Software interacts with hardware as a series of ones and zeros—switches being turned on and off—but these binary numerals can encode text, pictures, sound, video, and the complicated programs that make computers useful to human beings. Binary and decimal are not the only number systems used in computer science, and other number systems, like hexadecimal and octal can be even easier to work with than decimal. Boolean algebra allows us to abstractly represent the logic of computers and digital electronics. In the following unit, we'll have the chance to use computers for creativity as we turn to one of the most popular and useful applications ever created: Adobe Photoshop.

Important Vocabulary

- **Abstraction** – reducing information and detail to facilitate focus on relevant concepts
- **Application** – almost everything on the computer except saved files and the operating system, including word processors, photo editing software, web browsers, games, and music programs
- **ASCII** – American Standard Code for Information Interchange
- **Binary** – base-two, numeral system that uses zero and one
- **BIOS** – basic input/output system
- **Bit** – each numeral in the binary system, zero or one
- **Boolean Logic** – a branch of algebra where variables can only have two values: true or false
- **Byte** – eight bits

- **Central Processing Unit (CPU)** – carries out every command or process on the computer and can be thought of as the brain of the computer

- **Cloud Computing** – a type of distributed computing that involves using a network of remote servers to store, manage, and process data

- **Computer** – an electronic device that processes data according to a set of instructions or commands, known as a program

- **Core** – the central processing unit (CPU), the main memory, the motherboard, and the power supply

- **Decimal** – base-ten, numeral system that uses zero to nine

- **Digit** – each number in the decimal system, zero to nine

- **Distributed Computing** – a model that involves using multiple devices to run a program

- **Hardware** – the physical parts of the computer, including devices such as the monitor, keyboard, speakers, wires, chips, cables, plugs, disks, printers, and mice

- **Hexadecimal** – base 16, number system that uses 0-9 and a–f

- **Input and Output (I/O) Devices** – how the user interacts with the computer

- **Main Memory** – memory that temporarily stores information while it is being sent to the CPU, also called RAM

- **Motherboard** (logic board) – the standardized printed circuit board that connects the CPU, main memory, and peripherals

- **Nonvolatile** – does not need a power supply. Information is physically written to the device

- **Nybble (or Nibble)** – half byte, four bits
- **Operating System** – software that provides common services to other programs, manages hardware and software resources, and provides the visual representation of the computer
- **Parallel Computing** – breaks a program into multiple smaller sequential computing operations, some of which are performed simultaneously
- **Peripherals** – the input and output (I/O) devices and the secondary memory
- **POST** – power-on self-test
- **Power Supply** – converts AC electricity to the lower voltage DC electricity that is needed to power the computer
- **Random Access Memory (RAM)** – memory that can be retrieved or written to anywhere without having to go through all the previous memory
- **Secondary Memory** – used for long term storage and is physically changed when files are saved or deleted
- **Sequential Computing** – a model in which operations are performed in order, one at a time
- **Sequential Memory** – memory used to store back-up data on a tape
- **Software** – includes the operating system and the applications. It is usually stored on a computer's hard drive and cannot physically be touched. At the lowest level, it is a series of ones and zeros

- **Truth Table** – a table made up of rows and columns of Boolean variables and resulting Boolean expressions

- **Volatile** – needs a power supply. Turning off the power deletes information

---

2 – Pixels and Images

"Creativity is contagious. Pass it on."

- Albert Einstein

Introduction

The ability for anyone with a personal computer to easily and convincingly manipulate images may be one of the most significant changes of the last several decades, and the development of the graphical user interface was a huge step forward for making computers accessible to non-specialists. In this unit, we'll begin by introducing a couple of the ways in which images can be represented digitally before moving on to one of the most popular programs for manipulating these images, Adobe Photoshop. The ability of computers to display, create, transmit, and alter images has transformed our culture, not to mention the work lives of countless professionals. Programs like Adobe Photoshop have been central to this transformation. By the end of this unit, you should have a basic grasp of what digital images are and how you can create and change them.

Digital Images

Since the invention of the **graphical user interface (GUI)** this method of using visual icons to interact with an operating system has replaced most **text-based interfaces**, such as command-line interfaces, which rely purely on textual input from the user. Storing images and graphics as digital data has thus become paramount. GUIs have paved the way for the mice and touch-screen interfaces that have helped make computers more intuitive and user friendly. Graphics range from simple icons and text to large photographs and digital art. Adobe Photoshop and other software for creating and editing images have contributed to these graphical advances.

A **pixel**, short for picture element, is the basic unit of color on a computer display. The size of pixels on a screen varies depending on the display's resolution. If a display has more pixels then these pixels will be smaller and the image quality will be better. Scanning a picture or taking a digital photo turns an image into millions of individual pixels. In order to be understood by computers, these pixels are represented as binary numbers. Large pixels can make an image look blocky, a phenomenon known as **pixelation**. Contrary to what you may have seen in movies, there is no way to "enhance" these images since they do not contain the binary information for the missing pixels. When AI software, provided by Google and other companies, produces an enhanced digital zoom effect, it is doing so by combining digital information from multiple images taken at the same time.

All computers and digital televisions use these millions of pixels to produce images. Images created by using pixels are considered to be *raster* images. Sometimes, however, greater precision is needed, so *vector* images use mathematical formula to represent shapes. While this unit will deal with raster images, you should be familiar with the basics of vector graphics as well.

In a **raster**, a grid of pixels represents image data. Photoshop and many other photo editing applications deal mainly with such images. By modifying individual pixels, these applications can create effects, correct color, touch up photos, and improve images in a seemingly endless amount of ways. Photoshop can also deal with **vector** graphics, in which images are made from a combination of points connected by lines and curves. Adobe Illustrator was designed to create and edit vector images. In Photoshop two main uses of vector graphics are seen in the pen tool and in text. Vector graphics' advantage lies in their ability to scale. No matter how large an image becomes, a vector file can simply recalculate the shapes. For this reason, graphic designers work primarily in vector. They might need to create an image that will be used as a tiny icon or be scaled up and placed on a giant billboard. When raster images are scaled up, each pixel becomes larger, potentially leading to unacceptable levels of pixelation.

Some of the most common file types associated with raster graphics include the Joint Photographic Experts Group (.jpg/.jpeg), Portable Network Graphics (.png), Bitmap (.bmp), Graphics Interchange Format (.gif), Tag Image File Format (.tif/.tiff), and Photoshop Document (.psd). Popular vector files include Adobe Illustrator (.ai), Scalable Vector Graphics (.svg), Portable Document Format (.pdf), and Encapsulated PostScript (.eps). Although PDF and ESP files are vector formats, they can also contain raster images.

The simplest raster images are black and white. Each pixel in a black-and-white image takes up only a single bit since only two distinct values (black or white) are possible. A "0" could—and usually does—stand for black while "1" could represent white. You can think of this as a light being turned off (0) or on (1). Black-and-white images are therefore a fraction of the size of other formats and are used mainly for small logos or icons. Text could be stored as black-and-white raster images, but it would suffer from pixelation when the text is scaled up. For this reason, fonts are stored as vector files.

While black-and-white images have the advantage of size, they are limited to simple applications, like images of text or basic icons. In order to make shades of gray, different amounts of black and white can be mixed together. Using 8 bits (1 byte) to represent shades of gray yields 2^8 or 256 different possibilities. Even though these images only use one byte per pixel, they still take up eight times as many bits as black-and-white images.

Color images usually use even more bits per pixel. Color pixels can take up one byte, for a total of 256 colors (more on this in the next unit), but the human eye can distinguish over 10 million colors, so realistic images need to include at least that many possibilities. It is also important to know an image's main medium. Colors for displaying images on a screen differ slightly from those for printed images.

There are two main color models to consider: CMYK and RGB. **CMYK** is used for printing and stands for **c**yan, **m**agenta, **y**ellow, and black (key), where the number associated with each letter is the percentage of each color used. This is the **subtractive color** model, meaning white is the color of the paper and black is the combination of all the colors. Most printers have a separate black ink cartridge since it is more cost effective than combining the other three colors and then needing to replace these cartridges more often.

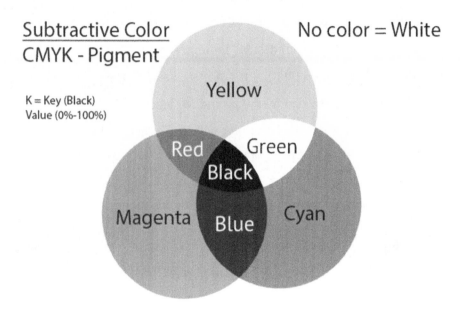

RGB (which stands for **r**ed, **g**reen, and **b**lue) refers to the color of light used in most monitors and screens. RGB is an **additive color** model. This means that no light is black and the combination of all light is white. Instead of using a percentage from 0–100, RGB (the 8-bit version) uses one byte (2^8 or 0–255) to represent each color. Since there are three colors, each RGB value (1 pixel) is 3 bytes of data (24 bits), much larger than the single bit each pixel in a black and white image uses. If the RGB value of a color is (255, 0, 0), all the red light is on and no green or blue light is on, so it would be a red pixel. Likewise, (0, 0, 255) would be blue. Using 24 bits to represent color gives 2^{24} possible combinations, that is 16,777,216 colors.

RGB color is often represented using decimal or hexadecimal. The decimal representation, which is seen above, is often placed in parentheses and sometimes preceded by the letters RGB: RGB (255, 255, 255). Converting these three decimal values to hexadecimal is very common, especially in web design. To represent 0 – 255 in hexadecimal, the values 00 (0) – ff (255) are used. These 6-digit hex codes are usually preceded by the pound (#) sign: #ffffff. At the lowest level, of course, the computer will read either of these values as the 24-bit binary code: 1111 1111 1111 1111 1111 1111.

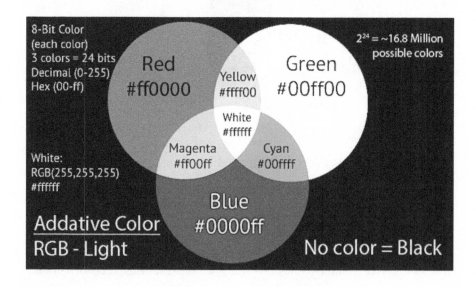

With over sixteen million different colors, RGB has many similar shades. So if a pixel has high red values, but still has low amounts of green or blue, it would still be a shade of red, like #d2150b or RGB (150, 50, 50). Likewise, shades of yellow could be made with higher amounts of red and green, like #999900 or RGB (230, 240, 42). Tertiary colors, like orange, can be created by having high values of one color and somewhere around 50% of another color. Orange is similar to yellow, but with less green light. Two shades of orange could be represented as #ff8000 or RGB (200,100,20). You can use the color picker tools built in to all the popular photo editors or available online to explore other colors. These tools will often display RGB and hex values as well. Some will display the closest corresponding CMYK color along with other color models such as HSB (hue, saturation, brightness) or Lab color, which fall outside the scope of this book.

Gray

As we have seen, equal amounts of red, green, and blue light create the illusion of white light, and equal amounts of no light create the color black. Since shades of gray come between black and white, it makes sense that approximately equal amounts of red, green, and blue light make gray. RGB (33, 33, 33) or #d2d2d2 would both be gray. The first is a dark gray, since it is closer to black (RGB (0, 0, 0)), and the second a lighter gray, since it closer to white (#ffffff).

Motion

Computers display more than just static images. There is movement on the screen, animations, and more. These effects are nothing more than pixels changing at a rapid rate. Computer screens modulate light by changing each one of millions of pixels many times per second. A display's refresh rate, measured in Hertz or cycles per second, determines how many times each pixel changes each second. 60 Hz, 75 Hz, and 144 Hz are common refresh rates, and higher end displays, such as those made for professional gamers, can reach rates of 240 Hz to 300 Hz. Film and TV most often use 24 Hz and 29.97 Hz, respectively. When such content is displayed on a 60 Hz monitor, for example, frames will need to be repeated or up-conversion applied by interpolating synthesized frames. This effect can cause "motion smoothing," which looks great for scrolling but is less than ideal for action movies or sports. Even good graphics cards cannot change millions of individual pixels simultaneously. Rather, each pixel is changed individually, usually from left to right and top to bottom. This happens so quickly that our eyes cannot distinguish it.

Common Sizes

Monitors and televisions come in a variety of standard sizes with set aspect ratios and numbers of rows and columns of pixels. HD and 4K refer to well-known standards. When someone says, "HD", they most likely mean Full High Definition or a width of 1,920 pixels by a height of 1,080 pixels (1920x1080). 4K usually refers to Ultra High Definition, which has four times the resolution of HD: 3,840 pixels wide by 2,160 pixels tall (3840x2160). HD adds up to 2,073,600 pixels while 4K displays four times as many, 8,294,400 total pixels.

Summary

In this unit, we learned about two of the most important ways to store and display graphics digitally, rasters and vectors. These graphic formats are used to encode everything from typefaces used in this book to the images on your HDTV. All these images—along with video, audio, and other information—can use massive amounts of data storage. In order to store and transmit all this data efficiently, compression is necessary. In unit three, we'll turn to this essential aspect of computing.

Important Vocabulary

- **Additive Color** – a color model where no light is black and the combination of all light is white, like RGB

- **CMYK** – color model used for printing. Stands for cyan, magenta, yellow, and black (key), where the number associated with each letter is the percentage of each color used

- **Graphical User Interface (GUI)** – an interface that uses images to represent a system's folders and files

- **Pixel** – short for picture element. The basic unit of color on a computer display

- **Pixelation** – when individual pixels are too large and the image begins to look blocky

- **Raster** – an image format that represents data in a grid of dots or pixels

- **RGB** – color model used for most monitors or screens. Stands for **r**ed, **g**reen, and **b**lue, referring to the color of light

- **Subtractive Color** – a color model where no light is white and the combination of all light is black, like CMYK

- **Text-Based Interface** – an interface purely made up of text input from the user

- **Vector** – an image format that represents data through a combination of points connected by lines and curves

---

2.5 - Adobe Photoshop

"You can hardly turn around and not see something that was done in Photoshop."

- John Knoll

Introduction

First published in 1990, Adobe Photoshop is considered to be the industry standard graphics editor and is the current market leader for commercial bitmap and image manipulation. Along with Adobe Acrobat, it is one of the most well-known pieces of software produced by Adobe Systems. It is used in most jobs related to the use of visual elements and is usually simply referred to as "Photoshop." Indeed, this program is so ubiquitous that its name is oftentimes used as verb, so you can "photoshop" a picture just as you would xerox a document or google who played Willow on *Buffy the Vampire Slayer* (although Adobe Systems would prefer that you didn't).

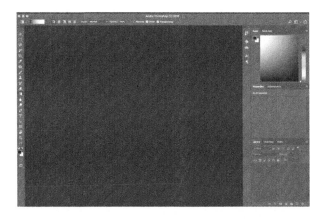

With Photoshop, a user can create and modify digital images or—rather—images in electronic form. Photoshop allows users to create original artwork, modify or combine existing pictures, add text or special effects to a webpage, and restore or touch up old photographs, among other tasks. The images to be modified can come from many places, including the web, digital cameras, or scanners. Once created or imported, the artwork can be modified. Users can rotate or resize these images. They can add text or change colors, and they can combine these images with others.

When you are ready to save an image, there are many possible file types to choose from. The most common are **.psd**, **.png**, **.jpg**, and **.gif**. Photoshop's native file format is **.psd**. Most other applications cannot read this format but can read the other three file types, which are also significantly smaller in size than the Photoshop format.

When modifying images in Photoshop, it's always a good idea to keep a copy of the original image in case you need to reuse the image or correct a mistake. To make sure the original image remains unaltered, use the *Save as...* command as soon as the image has been opened then choose a different name for the image that is going to be modified. This will create a copy of the original that will remain untouched and can be opened if there is ever a need to start from scratch.

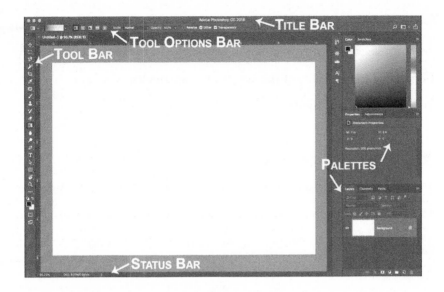

The **workspace** is the area between the tool option bar and the status bar. The workspace includes all the palettes, the toolbar, and the open document windows.

The **title bar** contains the name of the program as well as the close, minimize, and maximize buttons.

The **tool options bar** is located under the menu bar and shows more options for the selected tool from the toolbox. When a new tool is selected, the tool option bar will change to accommodate the selected tools. This option bar contains very useful additions to the selected tool that vary from tool to tool.

The **palettes** are small windows which start stacked up on the right side of the workspace. These palettes may be moved anywhere in the workspace and reordered as desired. The most useful palettes are the history palette and the layer palette, which show the last twenty actions performed and information about each layer in the image respectively. Located at the bottom of the screen, the **status bar** displays information about the file size and the active tool.

A layer is a part of the image that can be modified independently. They work much like those anatomy books that use clear pages to show the body's different systems, where each page can be folded back to show what the layer underneath looks like. Photoshop supports up to 8000 layers. Since the images that are blocked by other layers are still there, layers can contribute to very large file sizes. Images can be flattened to decrease file sizes. Flattening an image discards all image information that cannot be seen or is blocked. Other than .psd, most formats do not support layers, so saving in these formats will automatically flatten the image.

The **layer palette** shows the active layer by highlighting it. Multiple layers can be selected by holding down *shift* or *control/command.* To make layers easier to see, individual layers can be hidden. To do this, click the eye icon to the left of the 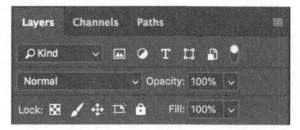 layer. Clicking the empty box where the eye used to be will make the layer visible again. Changing the layer's opacity to 0% from the top of the layer palette will achieve the same effect.

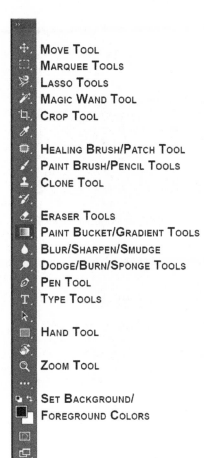

The **toolbar** contains frequently used Photoshop commands. Each tool is marked by a graphical representation of what the tool does. When the user moves the pointer over a tool, a screen tip will appear stating the name of the tool and the keyboard shortcut in parentheses. Some tools have other tools hidden behind them, denoted by a small triangle at the bottom right-hand corner of the tool. To see the hidden tools, hold down the pointer on the tool or right click.

When editing or combining images, you may need to take one piece of the image and either move or edit it.

Photoshop offers many ways to select parts of images, including the *marquee tool*, the *magic wand*, and three types of *lasso tools*.

The **marquee tool**, which has rectangular and elliptical options, should be used when the object is either a rectangular or round shape.

The **magic wand** can be used when the background is significantly different from the image. This tool automatically detects changes in color, so it is useful when an object is on a solid background. For other irregular shapes, the best way to select them is to use the lasso tools.

The three lasso tools are regular, polygonal, and magnetic. The **regular lasso** tool should be used for tracing the entire image by hand. When an object's edges are all straight, use the **polygonal lasso**. Like the magic wand tool, the **magnetic lasso** automatically detects changes in color. To use this tool, trace the object roughly, and the lasso will set anchors along the edges of the image.

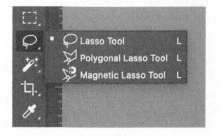

In the tool option bar for each of these tools, there are three useful options for making selections. The **new selection** tool is used when starting from scratch. The **add to selection** tool is used when a part is missing from the original selection or when another object needs to be added. The **subtract from selection** tool is used to remove part of the selection from the object.

There are also useful options in the **select** menu under the menu bar: **all, deselect**, and **inverse**. *All* selects the whole layer, *deselect* gets rid of any selections on the page, and *inverse* switches what is selected and unselected so that anything selected becomes unselected and anything unselected becomes selected. The ***modify*** option under this menu contains other useful options, which allow the selection to be expanded or contracted.

Now that an object has been selected, use the **move** tool to drag the selection from one image to another or to move it within the same image. If the move tool is not selected, then dragging the selection will only move the marquee or the dotted line, not the image selection itself. Right clicking inside the selection also allows for a new layer to be created from the selection, either by copying or cutting the selection.

Another way to select part of an image is to erase everything else. If an error is made, however, it can be hard to restore the deleted portion. The solution to this problem is masks. Masks allow you to crop out parts of a picture without modifying the pixels, so if a mistake is made, you can easily fix it by changing the mask, not the picture itself.

If a layer is locked as a background, double the click the layer in the layer palette, name it, and click ok to create a new layer. To begin masking, click the *mask button* that looks like a square with a circle cut out at the bottom of the layer palette. You can

also go to the *layer menu* and select *layer mask* and *reveal all*. Once a mask is on the layer, it can be effectively erased by painting the mask black.

Alternately, you can achieve the opposite effect by painting the mask white. It is important to set the paint brush being used to 100% hardness in order to create a perfect edge. Otherwise, the picture will appear to have a glowing edge. While using masks, use the *zoom tool* to get closer to the pixel level to get a crisp edge. Holding down *shift* and clicking with the paint brush will cause the dots to connect in a straight line, making the edges much crisper. See the list of useful shortcuts at the end of this unit.

Once an image has been masked, it is a good idea to duplicate this layer and lock the original as a master copy. If mistakes are made that cannot be reversed then a new duplicate can be made from the master copy. One way to create a duplicate of the masked layer is to hold down the *ctrl* key and click on the thumbnail of the mask. This selects the white area of the mask. Next make sure the thumbnail of the image is selected and select *Layer... New... Layer via Copy* from the menu bar. Double click the name of the original copy, rename it "master," then click the padlock icon at the top of the layer palette. Now that the master copy is locked, turn off the layer's visibility and drag it to the bottom of the layer palette.

Transformations are a way to scale, skew, distort, warp, flip, rotate, and shift the perspective on a layer. The most useful of these is scale. Scaling up usually does not work well since the layer can become pixelated. To scale down a layer select *Edit... Transform... Scale*, or use the keyboard shortcut for free transform: *ctrl/command + t*. To ensure

that the dimensions of the layer do not get distorted, hold down *shift* and grab the layer by a corner. When the transformation is complete, press *enter* to accept the changes or *esc* to cancel the transformation.

Filters are a way to edit an image's pixels to create a desired look or feel. There are several filters built into Photoshop. A downside of filters is that they do change the pixels, so the only way to remove a filter is to undo or step backwards. Smart filters store the original layer's information allowing these filters to be easily removed or changed. If a smart filter was not applied then there will be no way to recover the original image once the file has been saved and closed. Categories of filters include **artistic filters, stylize filters, render filters, noise filters, blur filters,** and **sketch filters.** All the filters can be seen by selecting the *filter*

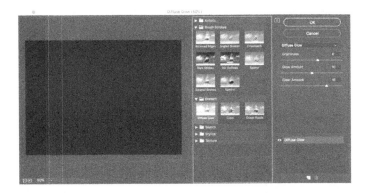

menu in the menu bar. Each category of filter includes many actual filters, such as **colored pencil, smudge stick, watercolor, pinch, ripple, wave, gaussian blur, tiles, clouds,** and **glowing edges**. Most of these filters have sub-menus as well that are indicated with an ellipsis. To see most categories at the same time, select *Filter Gallery*....

Layer styles are a good way to add effects to a layer. Unlike filters, layer styles can be turned on or off and changed as needed, even if the file has been saved and closed. Most of the options in layer styles affect the edge of the layer, so if a layer takes up the whole canvas, then layer styles might not be the best choice. A few useful styles are the **drop** 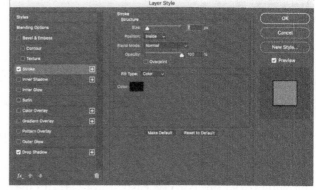 **shadow, outer glow, bevel and emboss,** and **stroke**. To bring up the layer styles window, double click to the right of the layer name on the layer palette or select *Layer... Layer Styles* from the menu bar. The check boxes can turn the styles on and off, and more options can be seen by clicking on the name of the style.

A gradient is a fill in which two or more colors blend together. The default gradient colors are the current foreground and background, but infinite possibilities can be selected by clicking on the preview of the gradient in the tool option bar. Gradients can also use transparency to achieve certain effects. In addition to colors, there are also five different types of gradients: linear, radial, angle, reflected, and diamond.

The type tool allows users to add text to Photoshop images, as in magazine and newspaper advertisements, which use to text to help get a message across to an audience. In such advertisements, many different fonts and colors can be used to emphasize certain parts of the overall image. In most cases, text or type should be used sparingly in Photoshop, as the overall file should mostly be the image itself. Text can be used to reinforce or complement an existing image. The text should be direct and large enough to be easily seen without being so large as to detract from the image itself.

There are three main font families: **serif, sans serif**, and **symbols**. A serif is a tail, or stroke, at the end of a character, and the word *sans* translates to "without." In other words, serif fonts contain a tail or stroke on most characters while sans serif fonts do not. Symbols are unique characters such as $, #, &, @, and *.

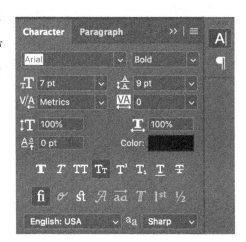

When the type tool is used, it automatically adds a new layer to the file. Simply click and type to add text. To change the size, color, or font of the text, highlight the text and change these things in the tool option bar at the top of the window. Selecting all the text in a layer can be done by double clicking on the thumbnail of the text layer in the layer palette. For more options to adjust the font, such as tracking or kerning, use the character palette, which looks like an A with a vertical bar to the right when collapsed. Many characteristics of fonts can be changed. One aspect that can be modified is the type spacing—the amount of space between characters. The type spacing can be set to monotype or proportional spacing. Monotype makes every character take up the same amount of space (*i* takes up the same amount of space as *w*). With proportional spacing, each letter takes up a different amount of space depending on the letter (this book uses proportional spacing!).

Summary

In this sub-unit, we've had a chance to start working with a program that is indispensable to many creative people. Photographers, graphic designers, magazine editors, and many, many other professionals use Photoshop every day in their careers. By mastering the tasks introduced above, you'll be well on your way to acquiring a set of skills with virtually unlimited potential.

Shortcuts

Ctrl + N:	New document
Ctrl + O:	Open document
Ctrl + S:	Save
Ctrl + A:	Select All
Ctrl + D:	Deselect
Ctrl + Z:	Undo
Ctrl + Alt + Z:	Step Backwards (Undo more than 1 step)
Ctrl + Shift + Z:	Step Forward (Redo more than one step)
Alt + Mouse Scroll:	Zoom in/out
Space Bar:	Hand tool (move around zoomed picture)
V:	Move tool
B:	Brush tool
G:	Paint Bucket/Gradient Tool
E:	Eraser
T:	Type Tool
M:	Marquee tools (rectangular, elliptical)
L:	Lasso tools (free lasso, polygonal, magnetic)
W:	Magic wand tool
D:	Set foreground/background to black/white
X:	Flip foreground and background color
[:	Make brush one size smaller
] :	Make brush one size larger
Shift + click:	Paint/draw straight lines
Ctrl + J:	New layer via copy
Ctrl + Click:	Select contents of the layer
(on layer thumbnail)	(white part of masks)

3 - Compressing Data

"No physical quantity can continue to change exponentially forever. Your job is delaying forever."

- Gordon Moore

Introduction

Today's world is filled with endless audio, images, videos, apps, and more. We're saving, sending, and downloading more data than ever before. Hard drive sizes may be increasing, but uncompressed files will still fill them up quickly. For example, an uncompressed, ninety-minute, HD (1080p) movie takes up approximately one terabyte of hard drive space. A common compression format for video called H.264 allows the same movie to be stored using only 65 gigabytes, fifteen times smaller than the uncompressed version. By using a video space calculator, it is easy to see how different formats (or numbers of frames per second) can result in dramatically different file sizes.

And that's just referring to space on a personal hard drive. Today, most of this digital information is sent over the Internet (which we will return to in unit six). The larger the file size, the longer it takes to download. Or even worse, streaming movies and TV shows may suffer from poor image quality or buffering! Given the amount of data sent over the Internet every second, it is important to keep file sizes small without compromising the quality of the material.

The choice of how to compress data will be determined by the trade-off between size and quality. If you aren't willing to sacrifice any quality then size of the compressed file will not be much smaller than the original. But if you just want a song to sound good on a personal speaker then some loss of quality is acceptable. Enough data can be removed from an mp3 to significantly reduce the file size without detracting from the listening experience.

In some cases, when data storage and bandwidth are plentiful, there is no need to shrink data, and files can be left **uncompressed**. That is, all the information from the original file will be kept in the same format without changing it a single—wait for it—bit. Anytime an analog signal is converted into digital some data is, by definition, lost, so when we talk about uncompressed data, we're referring to saving all the digital data that was captured by analog-to-digital audio converters or digital cameras.

In other cases, when smaller size is more important than perfect fidelity, it may be okay to lose some data. To achieve this smaller size, a **codec**, or a computer program that en**co**des or **dec**odes is used. When data is lost during this process, it is known as **lossy** compression. Ideally, the human eye or ear will not be able to detect this loss of data. An entire branch of psychology—**psychophysics**—deals with this this issue. A sub-branch called **psychoacoustics** focuses specifically on sound. These sciences study the relationship between stimulation and sensation and are essential for lossy compression techniques. To give an example, the human eye cannot see the difference between very similar shades of green, so when compressing an image, the computer may look at colors that are very similar and change them all to the same color. When dealing with millions of colors, this simplification could greatly reduce the file size, allowing it to load faster on websites or to be sent faster through email. For an audio file, this might mean a reduction in the sample rate (the number of values taken per second when converting an analog signal to a digital one) or bit rate (the number of total bits per second of audio). An audio file's sample rate could be reduced from 96 kHz to 44.1 kHz without the human ear (or really the human brain) being able to notice enough difference to justify the much larger file size. We'll return to audio compression in a moment.

In situations where a decompressed file needs to maintain all the original information it had before it was compressed then it is important not to lose any bits. When compressing text files or emails, for example, it is necessary to maintain all the original information, otherwise certain letters or words might be missing. This kind of compression is known as **lossless** compression, as it does not lose any data during compression. For some people who work with audio or video, lossless compression is essential. These professionals may need all the detailed information from the original file when mixing tracks or making precise changes to images. When working with most types of data, there are many options for both lossless and lossy compression.

On its own, data itself may not be useful. Additional information about the data is needed. This "data about the data" is known as **metadata.**

Even though the Greek prefix *meta-* means "after," it usually comes at the very beginning of the file. Most file types require metadata and have a strict set of rules about where it is located and how long it needs to be. Metadata may include title, author, keywords, date created, location where it was created, file size, height, width, and so on. Examples of what this metadata could look like will be discussed later in this unit.

Compressing Text

Given the rapidly falling costs of storage and bandwidth, large file sizes might not seem like a big deal, but as we will see in unit six, smaller file sizes are crucial when sending information thousands of miles over the Internet. Images, audio files, and videos are much larger than text files, generally speaking, but with the sheer number of emails and text messages sent every day, text compression is just as important. When compressing text, however, it is critical that no data is lost. Losing ten percent of an email might make it unreadable, so text compression will almost always be lossless.

As you'll recall from unit one, ASCII is a standard for encoding text in binary. In ASCII, each character is represented by eight bits (one byte). To figure out where any given character begins, just find bits that fall at an index that is divisible by eight. Since every character must be a block of eight bits, it is easy to locate one in the middle of a file. **Fixed-length code** contains blocks of code that are always the same size. One issue with this approach is wasted bits. For example, in

ASCII, the letter "A" is 100 0001, only seven bits. If the fixed length is 32 bits then all proceeding bits would need to be 0. The character "A" would then be 0000 0000 0000 0000 0000 0000 0100 0001.

An alternative to all these leading zeros is **variable-length code**, where each representation can be a different length. An early example of variable-length code is Morse Code. Samuel Morse, one of the inventors of the telegraph, realized that some letters, like "e" and "t", were more common than others, such as "j" or "z". For this reason, Morse Code represents "e" with a dot and "t" with a dash, while "j" and "z" are "dot-dash-dash-dash" and "dash-dash-dot-dot," respectively. Morse and others created this system in the 1830s, long before the invention of the digital computer, and telegraph operators could distinguish between letters by pausing between each one.

Unlike nineteenth-century telegraph operators, modern computers do not pause between commands. Instead, they use a specific type of variable-length code called **prefix-free code** (sometimes called prefix code). As in Morse Code, prefix-free code allows some characters' codes to be shorter than others. This can be seen in Huffman trees (more in a moment), where more common characters have shorter binary codes than infrequent ones. Prefix-free code works by ensuring that the beginning of each character does not match any other character. To see how this works, let's consider a simplified alphabet with only three letters (A, B, and C). In this example, if "A" starts with 0 and "B" with 1 then "C" could not start with 0 or 1 since those codes already stand for "A" and "B". Instead, "A" could be 0, "B" could be 10, and "C" could be 11.

Since characters are not evenly distributed in English or other languages, this creates the possibility of substantial data savings. It is more efficient to use a few bits for commonly used characters even if that means that less common characters need a dozen or more bits. For example, the letter "e" (which is used 13% of the time) shows up approximately 21,000 times in this book. The letter "j" (used less than .2%) only occurs about 250 times. So if it takes five bits to represent "e", that's 105,000 (5 x 21,000) bits total. If "j" needs 15 bits (to avoid repeating any prefixes), that's 3,750 (15 x 250) bits for a total of 108,750 (105,000 + 3,750). If we stuck with 8-bit ASCII values then "e" would take up 168,000 (8 x 21,000) bits and "j" would use 2,000 (8 x 250) bits for a total of 170,000 (168,000 + 2,000) bits. In this example, the fixed-length code is 56% larger than the variable-length option!

Prefix-free code is not just for text. It can be used whenever frequencies or patterns in code, known as redundancy, can be found. Finding redundancy—whether frequent colors in images, repeated sounds in audio files, or patterns of bits in applications—is the key to lossless compression.

In the early 1950s, an MIT doctoral student named David Huffman discovered the most efficient way to generate prefix-free code. His method uses **binary trees** (a tree that can have, at most, two nodes or "branches") sorted by frequency. Returning to the example above, this method does not assume the letter "e" to be most frequent. Instead, the code first scans all characters in the file and creates a tree starting with the least used characters at the bottom and working up to the most used at the top. Since the resulting tree has the most frequent characters on top, the "path" down the tree to get to them is shortest. With only two options at each node, the path taken to reach any character can be represented with a zero or one, ensuring that all characters will be prefix free. The result of this process is known as a **Huffman tree**.

The diagram below shows a Huffman tree created from the first paragraph of this book's foreword by CloudPainter's Pindar Van Arman (ignoring case).

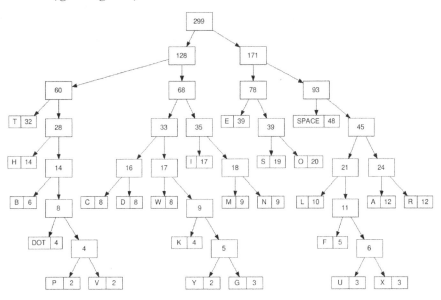

Each node is either the sum of all the characters below it, or it is a character, along with its frequency in the paragraph. To compress a character, locate it in the tree and starting at the top (there are 299 total characters in the paragraph) trace a path to it. Every time you take the left path, mark a zero. Every time you take the right path, mark a one. So to compress the first character, the letter "I", start from the top, take the left path, then the right twice, and finally the left to get 0110. The next character, "space," would be encoded as 110. Notice that "I", which appears 17 times, uses four bits while "space," which shows up 48 times, uses three. The letter "P", which only appears twice, converts to 0011110 for seven total bits. To decompress the resulting code, working in binary, simply follow the same pattern until a character is reached then start back at the top with the next character.

Huffman coding has been proven to be the most efficient way to compress text at the level of individual characters, but since this breakthrough, many more compression algorithms have been developed, most building upon Huffman's original insight.

In the example above, redundancy can be found in the encoding of individual characters, but redundancy can also be found in groups of characters, such as common words or patterns of letters, which may then be represented with a single character or symbol. Let's assume that every time the word "and" appeared in this book, it was replaced with a plus sign. The word "and" appears approximately 780 times in this book, taking up 2340 characters. If each "and" was replaced with a plus sign, it would take up only 780 characters. If the spaces before and after the word are included (_and_) that represents 3900 characters. Using a plus sign could reduce these 3900 characters to only 780 (plus six characters of metadata to tell the next user that the file was compressed). Imagine if other common words or letter groupings were changed into symbols. The letters "th" appear almost 4500 times in this book. Just by swapping "and" and "th" for symbols, we can reduce the length of this book by almost 8500 characters. That is more than five full pages! However, a key or **dictionary** in the metadata is needed to explain what words and letter groups were swapped. Otherwise, the result would be useless gibberish.

Without a dictionary, a message such as, "How much ♣ ♠a ♥ ♦if a ♥♠♦♣?" is nearly meaningless, but by following the dictionary (or metadata) to the right, the message can be decompressed to read: "How much wood could a woodchuck chuck if a woodchuck could chuck wood?"

♣	wood
♦	chuck
♥	♣ ♦
♠	could

The original message contains 58 characters and the compressed message contains 20 characters in the message and 20 characters in the key (metadata). This might not seem like much, but this simple compression made the file about 30% smaller. Imagine taking that uncompressed HD movie from the beginning of this unit and making it 30% smaller. The original file was a terabyte, so this would save about 300 gigabytes. Obviously, video cannot be compressed in exactly this manner, but there are even more ways to compress video to make it much smaller than the original. But think of how much text is on a computer: Word documents, emails, and more. If everyone tried to send dozens of uncompressed emails every day, Internet speeds would be at risk, a topic we'll return to in unit six.

In practice, however, even this simple compression could result in more dramatic savings. Since computers only deal with binary, these four symbols might actually be represented as 00, 01, 10, and 11. As seen earlier, characters in ASCII take up eight bits, so the word "wood" would be reduced from 32 bits to 2 bits. By combining this technique with Huffman trees, we can create prefix-free code in which the most common patterns have the shortest code.

Abraham Lempel and Jacob Ziv developed another kind of dictionary coding in an algorithm published in 1977, known simply a LZ77. Rather than defining a new dictionary, this algorithm references previous instances of the pattern in the code. So if "hello" (or rather the long string of bits that represents "hello") showed up earlier in the text, the algorithm would specify how for to jump back in the code to repeat the five bytes (if in ASCII) that made up "hello." To give a simplified example, this algorithm could use one byte to define first how far to go back in the code then how may characters to repeat or copy. So if "hello" appeared 30 characters before its subsequent instance, the binary code 11110101 could be used. The first five bits (11110) indicate how far to go back (30 characters) and the final three (101) indicate how may characters to repeat (the five characters of "hello"). In actual practice, multiple bytes would most likely be used to indicate a larger jump back.

Images use much more data than most text files. A 20,000-character document (more than 15 pages of this book) contains approximately 20,000 bytes (ignoring metadata), or about 19.5 kilobytes. Even a small 400-pixel-by-400-pixel image using 8-bit RGB color (that is eight bits per color per pixel) contains 160,000 pixels, which each require three bytes. That's a total of 480,000 bytes (ignoring metadata), or about 468.8 kilobytes. Most digital images are much larger and have millions of pixels, so it is important to compress them. There are two general ways to compress images. The first method is to find patterns, as in the above examples of compressing text. The second is to find unimportant information and toss it out. The first method is an example of lossless compression, but the second discards some data and is therefore lossy.

A simple example of converting binary code to a black and white image will help clarify how ones and zeros can become an image on a monitor. Black and white work well for this example, since they can be represented by a single bit. In this example, we will use zero for white and one for black (even though we know from unit two that black is represented as zero or off while white is on or all RGB colors). In addition to the color data, there must also be metadata to indicate such things as height and width.

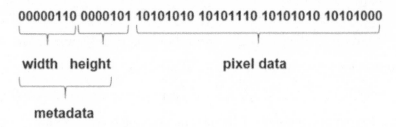

width   height   pixel data

metadata

In this example, the metadata are two bytes (sixteen bits) long and represent width and height, one byte for each. This kind of information is predetermined by the file type, and every file of this type must follow the same rules. If the first byte is converted from binary, it equals six, and the height is five. So, this image is six pixels by five pixels. The remaining four bytes of this file represent each pixel's color, black or white. Just like reading, start at the top left and fill in the

appropriate colors. Ones will be black and zeros will be white. Continue to the next row when needed. The result will say "Hi".

The image encoded through this process is uncompressed and uses a total of 48 bits, or 6 bytes. Lossless compression could reduce the file size. One way to reduce its size is to look for continuous streaks or runs of black or white pixels. Looking at the pixels from left to right, there are not many runs of black or white pixels since, most of the time, they alternate between single black or white pixels. But there are runs of alternating black and white pixels (one black then one white pixel), so, starting in the top left, there is a run of nine black-then-white pixels, then two black pixels (or one run of BB), then a run of eleven black-then-white pixels.

Expressed simply: 9BW, 1BB, 11BW. This expression can be converted to binary by specifying that six bits defines a run, where the first four bits indicate the length of the run and the final two bits represent the pattern. So 9BW would be 1001 01. 1BB would be 0001 00, and 11BW would be 1011 01. The entire image could then be encoded as 10 0101 0001 0010 1110, a total of 18 bits. With 16 bits of metadata, this image can be stored in 34 bits, almost thirty percent smaller than the uncompressed version.

This method of looking for redundancies or patterns as runs in the code is known as **run-length encoding**. A simple example of applying run-length encoding to text would be converting AAAAAAAAAABBBBBBBBBBCCCCC to 10A,10B,5C. In an RGB image, such encoding might specify that there are three-hundred red pixels in a row instead of using the three-byte code for red three-hundred times.

Compressing Images

Psychophysics plays an integral role in compression. Extensive research has been conducted on how humans see the color gray and how many shades human perception can distinguish. Different studies have concluded that humans can perceive anywhere from less than a dozen to several hundred distinct shades of gray. In a 2012 article published in the *Journal of the Royal Society Interface*, University of Cincinnati researchers found that humans can detect only about thirty distinct shades of gray. If this is true then what need is there to use a full byte to represent 256 shades? Thirty-two unique shades can be represented in binary using only five bits, which is 37.5% smaller. One way to compress a grayscale image, then, would be to throw out all but 32 shades of gray. **Discarding data**, like those other 224 grays, is lossy compression. There is no way to get that data back. The key to good lossy compression is finding the appropriate balance between size and quality. This technique can be used alongside lossless compression methods, such as run-length encoding to compress data even further.

Similarly, color images can be compressed by grouping similar colors and discarding the rest. Using eight bits for each red, green, and blue value yields over 16.3 (2^{24}) million possibilities, but the human eye can only distinguish about ten-million colors. Two colors only a few bits away from each other will appear identical, so compression algorithms for images take these similar colors and save them all as the same color. Most of the time this simplification should not change the quality of the image, but when these algorithms are too aggressive,

pixelation or color banding (which can be seen in the .gif file below) can occur.

A few common file formats that compress images include: .png, .bmp, .gif, and .jpg. Portable Network Graphics (.png) files use a lossless compression algorithm called Deflate which is a combination of LZ77 and Huffman Trees. Bitmaps (.bmp) use run-length encoding, which is also lossless. Graphic Interchange Format (.gif) uses a dictionary algorithm based on Terry Welch's additions to LZ78 (the successor to LZ77). Finally, Joint Photographic Experts Group (.jpg) files use lossy compression by breaking images into eight-pixel by eight-pixel blocks and using a method based on the mathematical operation *discrete cosine transform*. JPEGs remove high-frequency information in a process called quantization.

Compressing Video

Video compression uses similar techniques as the above examples. Since video is usually made up of 24 or 30 images displayed every second, one technique is simply to compress each image. This method is known as **intraframe** or spatial compression. If the frame-rate of a movie is 24 frames per second then 90 minutes of video would contain 2,160 individual images or frames, and each of these images could be compressed independently using the same algorithms applied to other images.

Similarities from one frame to the next can also be used to reduce file size. **Interframe** or temporal compression reuses redundant pixels from one frame to the next, so if eighty percent of the background barely changes, interframe compression simply leaves those pixels as is (or slightly moves or rotates them), only making changes to the twenty percent of pixels that do need updating.

Video compression is extremely important for streaming video, especially live video. Digital connections have a limited **bit rate**, the number of bits that can be processed per second. A typical home wireless connection might have a bit rate of twenty megabits per second (Mbps). As seen in unit one, the prefix "mega-" is used here to mean million, not 2^{20}, so twenty-million bits can be transferred per second. A 4k television displays 3,840 pixels by 2,160 pixels, a total of 8,294,400 pixels per frame. At 24 frames per second, one second of 4k video takes up 199,065,600 bits, requiring a dedicated connection speed of about 200 Mbps, not counting audio. If there is not enough bandwidth (the amount of bit rate available, discussed in unit six) then some data will not be transferred, resulting in compromised image quality or—even worse—buffering.

Compressing Audio

Lossless and lossy methods of compressing audio files use similar methods to those discussed above. Two well-known uncompressed audio file formats are .aiff in macOS and .wav in Windows. These formats are both actually containers that may package pulse-code modulation (PCM) streams, one method for converting analog signals into a digital form. Using metadata, these formats can also be used to contain compressed audio formats.

The fidelity of the digital representation encoded in a PCM stream is determined, in part, by the sample rate and the bit depth. As mentioned earlier in the unit, **sample rate** refers to the process of taking many digital representations of an analog signal. Sample rates in audio are generally measured in kilohertz (thousands of cycles per second), and common rates include 8 kHz for telephone calls, 44.1 kHz for CD and mp3 audio, 96 kHz for DVD audio, and 192 kHz for Blu-ray audio. Most humans cannot distinguish differences between sample rates that exceed 60 kHz, or 60,000 samples per second.

While sample rate refers to how often a digital representation is created, **bit depth** refers specifically to the number of bits used for each sample taken of the analog wave's amplitude. Common bit depths include 16 bit for CD audio and 24 bit for DVD audio. A 16-bit depth rate allows 65,536 (2^{16}) possible values for each sample and a 24-bit depth rate allows for about 16.8 million values.

The bit depth and sample rate of an audio file determine its bit rate. To determine the bit rate of an audio file, multiply its sample rate by its bit depth. A 44.1 kHz audio recording with a 16-bit bit depth translates to a 705,600 bits-per-second bit rate. Stereo audio uses two channels, so a stereo CD track recorded at these levels would have double the bit rate, 1,411,200 bits per second.

The sub-branch of psychophysics that deals with how humans hear sound, psychoacoustics, has found that humans can hear sound in a range from 20 Hz to 20,000 Hz (20 kHz), so there is little need to record frequencies outside this range. One lossy way to compress audio is to discard redundant data within this range, just like discarding color information when compressing image files. Other compression methods include changing the sample rate or bit depth, resulting in a lower bit rate. Two of the most popular lossy compression formats are .mp3 and .aac (made popular by Apple iTunes). The lossless methods discussed earlier can also be applied to audio files. For example, run-length encoding can be applied to periods of silence.

Summary

The modern world generates an enormous amount of information, and we don't just store this data, we move it around, oftentimes from one side of the planet to the other. Without compression, storing and moving all this information would be prohibitively expensive if not impossible. Compression, then, is one of the foundations of modern computing, and by gaining an understanding of the basics of compression, you have taken another step toward understanding how computers work—and work together—today. The ability of computers to display, store, transmit, and alter pictures and other forms of media is exciting, but an even more fundamental role of computing is the storage and processing of information, the subject of the next unit. Unit four will introduce two distinct ways of dealing with information: spreadsheets and databases. You will have a chance to begin learning

Microsoft Excel, a program that anyone who has ever worked in an office will be familiar with. Gaining familiarity with this surprisingly powerful application will prepare you for an even more surprising number of jobs.

Important Vocabulary

- **Binary Tree** – a data structure that can, at most, have two nodes or "branches"

- **Bit Depth** – refers to the amplitude of the analog wave and specifically to the number of bits used for each sample

- **Bit Rate** – the number of bits that can be processed per second

- **Codec** – a computer program that encodes or decodes

- **Dictionary** – a key in metadata explaining the instructions to encode or decode compressed data

- **Discarding Data** – a type of lossy compression that removes unneeded data with no way to get that data back

- **Fixed-length Code** – blocks of code that are always the same size

- **Huffman Tree** – a prefix-free binary tree that is the most efficient way to compress individual characters

- **Interframe Compression** –a video compression that re-uses redundant pixels from one frame to the next, also known as temporal compression

- **Intraframe Compression** – a technique used by compressing each frame of a video, also known as spatial compression

- **Lossless** – data compression that does not lose data during compression

- **Lossy** – data compression that loses data during compression

- **Metadata** – additional data about the main data, usually at the beginning of a file

- **Prefix-free Code** – a specific type of variable-length code that does not use pauses

- **Psychoacoustics** – a sub-branch of psychophysics that deals specifically with sound

- **Psychophysics** – a branch of psychology that focuses on the fact that the human eye or ear cannot perceive the loss of certain data

- **Redundancy** – finding frequencies or patterns in code

- **Run-length Encoding** – looking for redundancy or patterns as runs in the code

- **Sample Rate** – how often an analog signal is used when converting to digital, usually measured in kHz

- **Uncompressed** – all the information from an original file in the same format

- **Variable-length Code** – each data block can be a different length

4 – Storing Data: Spreadsheets and Databases

"The goal is to turn data into information, and information into insight."

- Carly Fiorina

Introduction

Data is everywhere. People have always collected information for multiple purposes. Data used to be relatively simple. Early humans recorded where they could find food and tracked weather patterns. With advancing technologies, however, data has become easier to collect and subsequently used for many more purposes. During the last fifty years, tracking television viewing habits has led to the current state of TV and targeted advertising. With this data, companies and advertising agencies can better target the consumers who are interested in their products. These companies save millions of dollars by not wasting money on consumers who are unlikely to buy their products while increasing sales by targeting their ads at more-likely-to-buy consumers. The existence of countless data sets creates a need for automated methods to store and retrieve information. This data could be someone's personal finances, which could be stored in a spreadsheet, or it could be a company's inventory and product details, for which a database would be more appropriate. Some data sets are so large or complex that an individual or small business alone could not gather, store, or analyze them using traditional methods. The field that deals with such information has come to be known as "big data."

Gathering Data

In the age of the internet, crowdsourcing has become a popular tool for gathering input or information from a large number of people. The practice of crowdsourcing offers new models for collaboration, connecting businesses or social causes with funding, and has even revolutionized the way we approach scientific research.

Crowdsourcing involves tapping into the collective intelligence of a large group of people to achieve a specific goal or solve a problem. With the help of technology, crowdsourcing has made it possible to obtain input from a diverse range of people from all over the world, in a matter of minutes.

One way that crowdsourcing has impacted scientific research is through the emergence of citizen science. **Citizen science** is a type of scientific research that is conducted, in whole or in part, by distributed individuals who contribute relevant data to research using their own computing devices. The individuals who participate in citizen science projects may not necessarily be scientists themselves, but their contributions can be invaluable in solving complex scientific problems. Citizen science projects have become increasingly popular over the years, thanks to the growing accessibility of technology and the internet.

While crowdsourcing and citizen science share some similarities, there are key differences between the two. Crowdsourcing typically involves obtaining input or information from a large number of people for a specific goal or project, while citizen science is focused on scientific research and the collection of relevant data. Additionally, the individuals who participate in citizen science projects may have a more active role in the research process, contributing to data collection and analysis, whereas crowdsourcing may involve more passive participation, such as providing feedback or suggestions. Nonetheless, both crowdsourcing and citizen science have opened up exciting new avenues for collaboration and problem-solving that were once unimaginable.

Visualizing data

Data is powerful, but humans cannot look at large datasets and immediately see trends or extract information from them. Fortunately, we now have powerful software and data libraries that can help us make sense of this information. A few clicks of a mouse or a couple lines of code can turn thousands of numbers on a spreadsheet into a line graph with trend lines, an interactive 3-D model, or an animation. Visual display allows more information to be displayed, and multiple datasets can be combined to reveal the bigger picture. Modern computers make these tasks easier, but data visualization long predates the transistor. Two celebrated, historical examples of data visualization are Charles Minard's map of Napoleon's 1812-13 Russian Campaign and John Snow's mapping of cholera outbreaks in 1854.

Minard's map skillfully displays several pieces of data: the size of the French army, location using latitude and longitude, distance traveled, direction traveled, relative dates, and temperature. The infographic shows the size of the army with the line's thickness and indicates where troops broke off from the main force. As the line moves from left to right, the thinning line shows the loss of troops from battles or the elements. Moscow lies on the right side of the map, which is where the troops turn back and make their way back west, as seen in the thinning black line. The sub-freezing temperatures faced on the return trip can be seen at the bottom. The black line briefly widens as troops rejoin from previous offshoots but thins again at the crossing of the Berezina River. The contrast between the original line and the black line on the left side of the map is devastatingly effective at showing how this campaign ended. Viewed separately, map coordinates, dates, temperatures, and troop numbers would not tell the same story, and piecing together dates and locations with temperatures would be tedious. It's not the whole story, but this infographic displays an easy to understand summary of the campaign, all without the help of a computer.

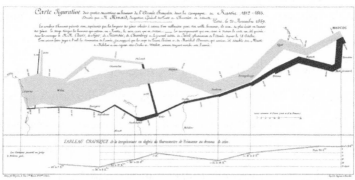

Infographic of Napoleon's 1812 Russian campaign - Charles Minard, 1869

John Snow, an English Physician, knew something when he mapped the locations of cholera cases, eventually showing that the cases stemmed from a contaminated water supply. Before this discovery, cholera was not understood to be water-borne, and for this reason, John Snow is now considered to be one of the founders of modern epidemiology.

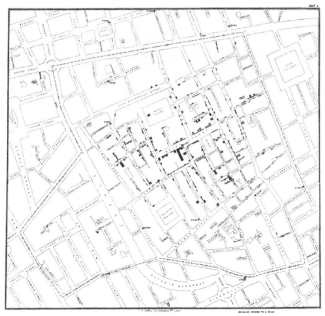

Mapping a cholera outbreak - John Snow, 1854.

Today both Minard and Snow might be called data scientists. Data science is a relatively new field that uses a variety of methods, including algorithms, to make sense of structured and unstructured data. Popular programming languages like Python and R have libraries to assist in data wrangling, visualization, and modeling.

Misleading Data

Data visualization is powerful, but it can be dangerous if misinterpreted, misused, or manipulated. Countless examples of misleading charts can be found in advertising, news outlets, politics and anywhere data is displayed. One of the most common misinterpretations of data is the assumption that correlation implies causation. Just because one set of data trends in similar fashion to another does not mean that one caused the other or vice versa. While causation may in fact be present, it cannot be found from this data alone. One admittedly ridiculous example of this would be noticing that the louder you sing in the shower, the higher the stock market rises. You could measure and chart your singing volume on the same graph as the daily gain or loss of the stock market, and they might look very similar. But does this mean that your singing is causing fluctuations in the market? Depending on who you are, probably not. Could it be that you're singing more loudly because you just made a lot of money? Maybe, but more evidence is needed.

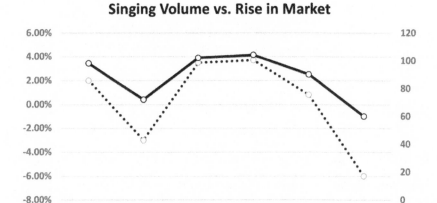

Correlation does not imply causation

Another common way for charts, especially bar graphs, to mislead is through manipulating the range of the axes. The two graphs below visualize identical data. The only change is that the range of the left graph's y-axis is from 48.95% to 49.45% while the right graph's y-axis ranges from 0% to 100%. In the left graph, B appears to be three times taller than A while the right graph more honestly shows B as only 0.3% higher than A. Without labels on the graph, people might overlook the values on the y-axis. Both graphs are technically correct, but the left graph uses techniques that are likely to deceive the viewer. When looking at data—assuming it is factual—make sure to check the axis and labels to avoid making snap judgements or assumptions.

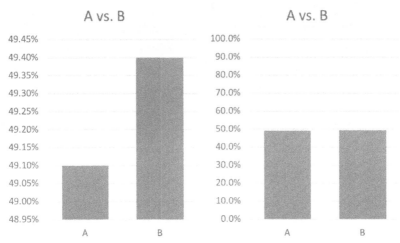

*The graph on the left makes it appear that **B** is 3x better than **A**
The graph on the right clearly shows that **B** is only .3% better than **A***

Simpson's paradox can also lead to misinterpreted data. This phenomenon occurs when groups of data individually trend in one direction, but when they are combined, this trend disappears or is reversed. Simpson's paradox may be found in medical trials and the social sciences and can be the result of poorly designed experiments or—as in the previous example—be misused to mislead for personal or financial gains.

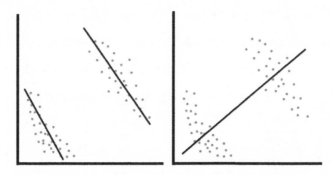

An example of Simpson's paradox - Individually each set trends downwards (left), but when plotted together the trend reverses (right)

Implying causation that is not supported by the evidence, manipulating the values of an axis, and Simpson's paradox can all lead to factual data being incorrectly understood. It is therefore important to look deeper into the data and not draw quick conclusions based on a glance at a pretty graph. It is also important to consider data's source. Who benefits from these results? Unfortunately, completely fabricated data also exists, so it is essential to find reputable sources. Does the latest viral infographic on Instagram originate from a legitimate source? Can you even tell who created it before it was shared around?

Spreadsheets

Prior to the introduction of electronic spreadsheets, accounting and bookkeeping had to be done by hand on paper—a slow and laborious process. With the introduction of VisiCalc on the Apple II (in 1979) and Lotus 1-2-3 on the IBM PC (in 1983), these tasks quickly became computerized. Since then, the use of spreadsheets has spread well beyond financial record keeping. Microsoft Excel gradually supplanted Lotus 1-2-3 and—with the release of version five in 1993—became the overwhelmingly dominant spreadsheet application. The program features an intuitive interface and graphing tools and is capable of a high level of calculation. These features—along with aggressive marketing and its bundling as part of Microsoft Office—have made Excel one of the most popular computer applications to date.

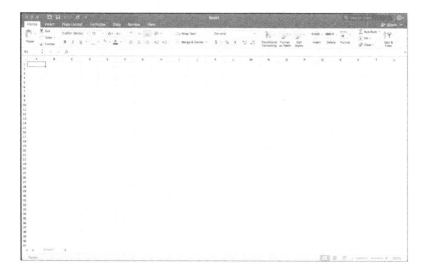

A spreadsheet is basically a grid used to store information, usually numbers. This grid consists of rows and columns. **Rows** go from left to right like rows of seats in a movie theater and are labeled using numbers starting at one. In Excel, there are over one million possible rows. **Columns** go from top to bottom like the columns that used to hold up Greek ruins. Columns are labeled using letters starting with A. When more than 26 columns are present, double letters are used, continuing with AA, AB, AC, AD, etc., then triple letters starting with AAA, AAB... all the way until XFD.

Each individual piece of the grid—where the rows and columns intersect—is called a **cell**. Each cell is labelled with the column letter followed by the row number so that A1 is the cell at the top left of the spreadsheet. Three basic items can be placed into the cells: labels, constants, and formulas. A **label** is text that describes some part of the spreadsheet, such as a name or amount. Labels are not meant for the computer but rather for humans to better understand the information in the cell. A **constant** is any number that the user enters into the spreadsheet. It will not change unless the user changes it manually. A **formula** is an equation that can perform calculations on existing cells. All formulas must start with an equal sign. Examples of formulas are: *=5 + 6*5* or *=2*F4 - A7*. Notice that F4 and A7 are cells, so whatever numbers are in these cells will be subtracted or multiplied. If this cell contains a label or has been left blank, then errors may occur.

Functions

Excel has many built-in functions that can help manipulate data. Some of these functions include finding minimums or maximums, calculating averages or sums, performing trig functions, and carrying out conditional statements. There are more than two-hundred functions in Excel. They can be found either by knowing the name of the function or by going to *Formulas... Insert Function...* A list of functions will then pop-up that can be narrowed down by searching or selecting a category. Notice that all functions (like formulas) begin with an equal sign.

At the bottom of the window, there will be a brief description on what the function does. A more detailed description will be given when the function is selected.

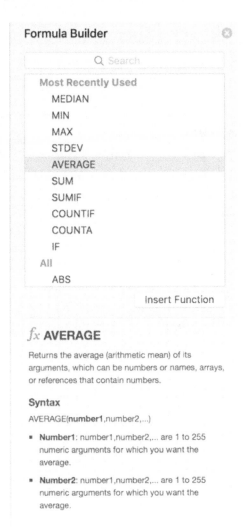

Formula Builder

Q Search

Most Recently Used
MEDIAN
MIN
MAX
STDEV
AVERAGE
SUM
SUMIF
COUNTIF
COUNTA
IF
All
ABS

Insert Function

fx **AVERAGE**

Returns the average (arithmetic mean) of its arguments, which can be numbers or names, arrays, or references that contain numbers.

Syntax

AVERAGE(**number1**,number2,...)

- **Number1**: number1,number2,... are 1 to 255 numeric arguments for which you want the average.
- **Number2**: number1,number2,... are 1 to 255 numeric arguments for which you want the average.

The following chart shows some useful functions and how they look when entered into the cell:

Name	Description	Sample Code	Appears in Cell
AVG	Finds the average from a list of numbers	=AVG(A1, A4, A6, A8)	4.75
MIN & MAX	Finds the minimum/maximum value of a list of numbers and returns that number	=MIN(D1:D9) = MAX(B13:B23)	37 104
COUNT	Counts how many cells have numerical data	=COUNT(A1:K30)	29
COUNT A	counts all data, text included	=COUNTA(A1:K30)	46
COUNT IF	Counts the number of cells that meet a given condition	=COUNTIF(A1:A32, ">75")	23
SUM	Adds up all the values and returns the answer	=SUM(A1,A5,B3,D5)	73

IF	This function can return different things depending on whether the condition is met. The first item after the condition is displayed if it is true and the second if false	=IF(B1<C1,"You win", "You lose")	You lose
IFS	This function allows for multiple if statements. The parameters alternate between the condition and the value to be displayed. As soon as one condition is true, the function returns the value and is complete.	=IFS(B1>=90, "A", B1>=80, "B")	B

Embedding Functions

Functions and formulas can work together. Some functions can even be embedded—or inserted—into other functions. For example, if you wanted to find what group of cells had the highest average, then you might write it like this:

=max(average(A1:A20), average(B1:B20), average(C1:C20))

Formatting

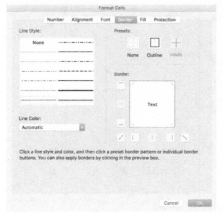

Formatting is a way to make the data in a spreadsheet more visually appealing. This can be done by changing the look of numbers; altering the font, color, or size; adding borders; or aligning the text in different ways. By right clicking on a cell, or selecting *Formatting... Format Cells...* under the *Home* tab, the *format cells* window will appear. There will be six tabs to choose from at the top of this window. These tabs can easily be mastered by experimenting with the different options.

Conditional Formatting

Excel has some built-in formatting tools that will automatically perform calculations for the user. Some of these tools can highlight cells that meet specific criteria, such as equaling a value, being greater than a certain value, or being less than a certain value. Other tools can highlight cells that are in the top or bottom five or ten or that have any given value. It can also be done with percentages. Conditional formatting can also turn cells into mini graphs using data bars or different color schemes. These graphs are determined by the highest and lowest values and can be modified by going into *more options*.

To remove conditional formatting, highlight the cells and select *Clear Rules* in the conditional formatting menu.

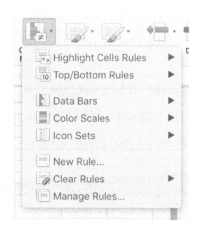

Auto Formatting

Excel also includes several pre-made templates that can change a spreadsheet's look automatically, eliminating the need to change colors and borders by hand. To use a template, select the cells that are to be formatted, then select *Formatting... Format as Table...* from the *Home* menu bar.

Charts

Excel can create charts and graphs from the data in a spreadsheet. There are several different charts that can be created, the most common being the bar, pie, and line charts. Under each chart type, there are sub-types that can give the graph more effects, such as making it three-dimensional or showing relationships throughout the data. Remember that a line graph shows change over time. To choose the desired type of chart, select it under the *Insert* tab.

Before a chart type is selected, the data range needs to be chosen. This can be done by highlighting the cells that contain the data. To select cells that are not adjacent, choose the first set of cells, then hold down the *ctrl* key and select the next set. Once you have selected the data, click on the type of chart as shown in the picture above. The *Design*, *Layout*, and *Format* tabs that will appear when you click on the chart can be used to add titles as well as axes names, legends, and data labels. Some of these tabs are shown below.

Printing

There are many options for printing an Excel document. These options can all be found under *File… Page Setup…*

Under the *Page* tab, the orientation of the page can be set (either vertical or horizontal). The spreadsheet may also be scaled to fit on a desired number of pages. Another useful tab is the *Sheet* tab. The most useful item under this tab is the *Gridlines* checkbox under the *Print* section. When checked, this tab will display the lines in the spreadsheet. Excel does not show gridlines by default.

Spreadsheet applications are essential tools for organizing and calculating. As the most popular of these programs, Excel is ubiquitous in offices around the world. Spreadsheets make calculating budgets, organizing large events, or managing groups of people

much more manageable. Mastering the powerful features of Excel will serve you well in an enormous variety of careers.

Databases

Another format for storing and processing data is the database. A database is simply an organized collection of data stored in tables. Like spreadsheets, these tables are made up of rows and columns. Throughout these tables, the data is consistent. In a database, **consistency** refers to the fact that information in one table does not contradict itself in any other table throughout the database. So if one table in a bank's database states that you have $5 in your account then any other tables with your information must also state that you have $5.

Inconsistencies commonly occur in mutual relationships. For example, a school's database might have separate tables for individual students and for class registrations. If a student's table indicates that they are enrolled in CS301-3 then CS301-3's table of enrolled students must also list this student. One cannot be true without the other. Fixing this inconsistency should be pretty easy, but others may not be so simple.

Inconsistencies could be introduced in a database when a program terminates before completing all transactions. The database might not know which transactions it needs to run again when the program starts back up. Let's say you try to buy something on Amazon but your transaction is interrupted after your credit card is charged but before this information gets sent to Amazon. On restart, the database might again seek to withdraw from your account, double charging you. To prevent this issue, all transactions must be idempotent. **Idempotency** means that an operation will result in the same end result no matter how many times it is performed. This property is seen in **write-ahead logging**, in which all changes are written and saved to a log before they're applied to the database, so all the components involved in a transaction need to be carried out before the entire transaction is considered complete. Such transactions are known as **atomic transactions** since they cannot be broken down while being executed. In the Amazon example, the atomic transaction would be all the steps involved in making the sale. If every part does not finish then none will. One way to prevent such inconsistencies is to work backward in the write-ahead log. This method is known as a **rollback**, returning back to the state before the write-ahead log began.

Inconsistencies may also arise if multiple transactions modify data from the same cell simultaneously. One way to prevent this error is to lock the cell that needs to be modified. If, for example, an account balance needs to be altered by two separate transactions then the first transaction would lock the row, make its changes, and then unlock the row. After the row is unlocked, the second transaction would then do the same. A **deadlock** can occur when two transactions are trying to lock the same row and neither can continue until the other is complete. In such cases, it is essential to have the ability to rollback one of the transactions to let the other finish.

The **two-phase commit protocol** provides another way to check whether multiple rows are free to use. This protocol is a standardized way to make sure all data can be written without any inconsistencies. The first phase is a check to see if all processes can be completed. If they can be written without issue then the second phase will commit all processes. If not, this phase will rollback.

When using databases, it is oftentimes convenient to use multiple tables to store data that is connected in some way to other data. A **relational database** can be used for this purpose. Relational databases have multiple tables that are connected or related through the use of unique **keys**, a column holding a unique value that distinguishes each record from all others. A school's database might include one table that contains students, using their unique student ID numbers as their keys. Another table might contain courses, using unique course IDs as keys. A **virtual table** or view could be created from this information using Structured Query Language or SQL (more in a second). Virtual tables are temporary tables made up of parts of other tables that help to reduce redundant data. In this example, a student's record might contain the unique course ID of a class they are taking, and this course ID might serve as a key in another table (perhaps storing more detailed course information). A new virtual table could then use the course ID to combine parts of the student's table, such as their schedule, with parts of the courses table, like teacher, meeting location, time, etc. This way the student record only needs the course ID to retrieve all the data about the course without the need to independently store all course data for each student. Course updates can then be made simply by modifying the course's table. There is no need to separately update this information for each and every enrolled student.

SQL

Structured Query Language (SQL) is the language used to manage, access, and manipulate relational databases. Although tables can be modified, this section focuses on creating virtual tables by accessing certain elements or combining parts of multiple tables. SQL ignores white space and is not case-sensitive. Statements can therefore be broken into several lines for easier readability, and "SELECT" is equivalent to "select." The lack of case sensitivity refers only to keywords, not to table names, columns, or text contained in an entry. Some of the most important keywords in SQL are discussed here: SELECT, DISTINCT, FROM, WHERE, LIKE, ORDER, BY, ASC, DESC, LIMIT, JOIN, and ON.

Assuming you are already connected to the proper database, you can access the *class_year* of all students from a table called *students* with the following query:

```
SELECT class_year FROM students;
```

This would return every student's class year, including duplicates, which could become an issue for databases with hundreds, thousands, or even millions of records. The result would also be unsorted. To get unique values that are sorted in descending order, use DISTINCT to only list unique values and ORDER BY to sort the data. Following that with DESC will put the results in descending order while ASC will give you ascending order.

```
SELECT DISTINCT class_year
FROM students
ORDER BY class_year DESC;
```

In order to limit the results to a certain number of rows, use LIMIT. The asterisk (*) can be used to specify all columns of a table. This example returns all columns from the first twenty rows.

```
SELECT *
FROM students
LIMIT 20;
```

If you only need the columns *first_name, last_name,* and *gpa* from the 100 students with the lowest GPAs, this statement could be used:

```
SELECT first_name, last_name, gpa
FROM students
ORDER BY gpa ASC
LIMIT 100;
```

It is common to want only records that match specific criteria, which can be achieved using the WHERE keyboard. If you only want the records from students with the last name "Smith," the equal sign can be used to check for an exact match:

```
SELECT *
FROM students
WHERE last_name = 'Smith';
```

The logical operators AND, OR, and NOT may also be used in conjunction with the WHERE keyword. In the following example, only records of students with the first name Sue who have a GPA of 4 will be shown:

```
SELECT *
FROM students
WHERE first_name = 'Sue'
AND gpa = 4;
```

Often, when querying a database, you don't want to match an exact string. Rather, you're seeking entries that contain a specific word or start with a certain letter or letters. Such partial matches can be indicated using the keyword LIKE paired with wildcard characters. Two common wildcard characters are the percent sign (%) and the underscore (_). "%" represents zero or more unknown characters, and "_" represents exactly one unknown character. "LIKE 'W%'" would return entries of any length that start with a capital "W." "LIKE '%ing'" would return only entries ending in "ing." "LIKE '%and%'" returns any string containing "and." "LIKE 'A%a' returns entries that begin with capital "A" and end with lowercase "a." The following query shows all students with a first name beginning with "A" and a last name ending in "y":

```
SELECT *
FROM students
WHERE first_name LIKE 'A%'
AND last_name LIKE '%y' ;
```

The "_" wildcard is less commonly used but works in a similar fashion. It represents exactly one character—not zero and not more than one. "LIKE 'T_m'" would return strings like "Tim," "Tom," and "Tum" but exclude "Tram" and "Totem." These wildcards can work in tandem. The following query will show names like "Tim," "Tom," "Timmy," and "Tomas":

```
SELECT *
FROM students
WHERE first_name LIKE 'T_m%';
```

To combine entries from two or more tables, use the JOIN keyword.
There are several kinds of join statements. The default type is the inner
join, which returns rows where both tables include the specified data.
The ON keyword indicates how the tables being joined are related.
ON specifies the column relationship between the original table and
the one it is being combined with. In the following example, the *student*
table is joined with the *sports* table using a common link, the student's
social security number. Then only students on the dance team who are
in the 10th grade are shown in alphabetical order by their last name.

```
SELECT *
FROM students
JOIN sports
ON students.ssn = sports.ssn
WHERE students.class_year = 10
AND sports.team = 'dance team'
ORDER BY students.last_name ASC;
```

Aliases can be used to shorten table names. In lines three and four of
this example, *st* and *sp* are created as aliases for *students* and *sports*,
respectively, so anytime the *students* table is referenced, the shorter *st* can
be used. Another way to make columns more user friendly is to rename

them in the new table. In this example, the keyword AS is used when selecting columns to rename *last_name* to *Last* in the new table.

```
SELECT st.first_name AS First,
st.last_name AS Last, sp.team
FROM students st
JOIN sports sp
ON st.ssn = sp.ssn
WHERE st.class_year = 10
AND sp.team = 'dance team'
ORDER BY st.last_name ASC;
```

Aggregate functions in SQL can be applied to several values in a column. Many of these will be familiar from the spreadsheet section above: *min*, *max*, *sum*, *avg*, and *count*. For functions, parentheses are used to specify the columns being aggregated. To find the average GPA of all students:

```
SELECT avg(gpa)
FROM student;
```

Scalar functions return data from a single value. Useful scalar functions include *round*, *upper/ucase*, and *lower/lcase*. Strings are case-sensitive, so a search for "Bob" would not match to "bob." *lower* or *lcase* provides a solution to this problem. In this example, we use the *lower* function on the entry than compare it to a lower-case string:

```
SELECT *
FROM students
WHERE lower(first_name) = 'bob';
```

This section only scratches the surface of what SQL can accomplish. These keywords are useful when searching for data, sorting and filtering results, and even renaming column headers. These functions can help with case-sensitivity and rounding long decimals, and other tasks. There are many other keywords and functions that can be used to create new data, modify existing data, and remove unwanted data.

As with any computing system, **fault-tolerance**, the ability of a system to continue to run properly even if one piece fails, is an imperative property for databases. The protocols discussed above make sure that databases can continue to work properly even when errors occur.

Big Data

Big data often refers to sets of data that are larger than a consumer software application can handle. This could be data collected from hundreds of sources, including mobile phones, software, web browser logs, cameras, and wireless networks. A few key features of big data are the volume of the data, the rate at which it is collected, the variety of types, and the fact computers can "learn" from it. The volume is important since it is not a sample of data from different groups of people: It is all the data from all the people, so there is—in principle— less room for error. The rate at which data is collected is also important since, given the speed of processors and fiber optics, the data is in real-time. Big data's variety allows text, audio, video, and more to be collected simultaneously and analyzed. This allows the data to be seen from different angles, making the results even more accurate. Finally, computers can see trends and patterns in this data that would take humans many lifetimes to sift through. Not only can computers see the trends, but they can also learn from them and use them when analyzing similar data in the future. Big data is very powerful and companies pay top dollar to obtain it.

In 2012 Facebook bought Instagram for one-billion dollars. That is billion—with a "B." Any programmer at Facebook easily could have designed an app that did the exact same thing as Instagram, probably with improvements. So why pay one-thousand-million dollars for an app? At the time, Instagram had thirty-million users, and it had a lot of data about those thirty-million users. This data included how often they were on the app, how long they used the app per session, what profiles they looked at, what pictures they liked, all their search results, and more. The app itself was not worth one-billion dollars, but the large data set Instagram collected and the site's daily active users were worth that much to Facebook.

Big data is seen in many other industries, including government, education, media, healthcare, banking, real estate, retail, and more. The app Waze (acquired by Google for almost one-billion dollars) used to collect every user's data, even when the app is not open. When installed, the user gave permission to always use their location. If the user's geolocation is on a road then the app can record their speed. This information can be used to predict traffic and help reroute other users in real-time.

Summary

It would be hard to underestimate the role data has come to play in our economy and society. Spreadsheets have gone from being the cumbersome physical tools of accountants to essential and flexible digital tools for most office workers. Databases store untold amounts of data, replacing everything from the library card catalog to student schedules to banking records and making entirely new kinds of records possible. These tools and their more sophisticated successors have made big data possible. In the final unit, on the impact of computing, we'll discuss some of the social and economic effects of this turn to big data. In the following unit, however, we'll consider the available tools for keeping all this sensitive data secure, including encryption and other defenses against malicious hackers.

Important Vocabulary

- **Atomic Transaction** – transaction where all components must be carried out before the transaction is considered complete such that all occur or none occur
- **Big Data** – sets of data that are larger than a consumer software application can handle

- **Citizen Science** – a type of scientific research that is conducted, in whole or in part, by distributed individuals who contribute relevant data to research using their own computing devices

- **Consistency** – refers to the fact that information from one table does not contradict itself in any other table throughout a database

- **Crowdsourcing** – tapping into the collective intelligence of a large group of people to achieve a specific goal or solve a problem

- **Deadlock** – when, in a database, two transactions are trying to lock the same row and neither can continue until the other is complete

- **Fault-tolerance** – the ability for a system to continue to run properly even if one piece fails

- **Idempotency** – when an operation results in the same end result no matter how many times it is performed

- **Keys** – a database column that holds a unique value that distinguishes each record from others

- **Relational Database** – a database that has multiple tables that are connected by the use of unique keys

- **Rollback** – returning back to the state of a database before the write-ahead log began

- **Simpson's Paradox** – a phenomenon that can occur when multiple groups of data trend in one direction but when combined with other sets the trend disappears or reverses

- **Structured Query Language (SQL)** – the language used to manage, access, and manipulate relational databases

- **Two-phase Commit Protocol** – a standardized way for databases to make sure all transactions are able to write without any inconsistencies before committing

- **Virtual Tables** – temporary tables that are made up of parts of other tables that help in reducing redundant data

- **Write-ahead Logging** – a method for avoiding inconsistencies in which all transactions are written and saved to a log before they are applied to a database

---

5 - Protecting Data: Heuristics, Security, and Encryption

"If you put a key under the mat for the cops, a burglar can find it, too. Criminals are using every technology tool at their disposal to hack into people's accounts. If they know there's a key hidden somewhere, they won't stop until they find it."

- Tim Cook

Introduction

When it comes to using computers and networks, good security practices are no longer optional. Data breaches, distributed denial of service attacks, viruses, worms, Trojan horses, and ransomware have all been in the news in recent years. Major cities, financial firms, hospital systems, and even national militaries have all faced such attacks. Administrators of these systems have an obligation to take appropriate measures to ensure their security, but individual users should also take steps to secure their accounts by adopting best practices, such as using strong and unique passwords. Of course, the best password in the world won't keep data secure if it is stored and transmitted in the clear. That's where encryption comes in. Encryption can be a controversial topic, but it is essential for everything from secure online banking to private communications, and it is a major topic of this unit.

Heuristics

In programming, a **heuristic approach** is an approach that gives results that are "good enough" when an exact answer is not necessary. This is seen in the famous **traveling salesman problem (TSP)**, in which a hypothetical salesman is given a list of cities and the distances between them and is tasked with mapping out the shortest route for visiting each city and returning home to the original city. With only a few cities, the problem is simple, but it becomes exponentially more difficult as more cities are added. The TSP is **computationally hard**, meaning even a computer would take too long to find the exact solution. An instance using 85,900 "cities" was solved in 2006, but it took the equivalent of a computer running 24 hours a day for 136 years. The amount of time and computational power to find this solution was out of proportion to the result. It would have been more sensible to find a "good" route in a much shorter amount of time.

While calculating the best solution is difficult, it is easy to quickly check if any given solution is best. For this reason, the TSP is an **NP problem** ("nondeterministic polynomial time"—a concept which lies outside the scope of this book), meaning it can be verified—but not solved—in polynomial time (roughly meaning a feasible or efficient amount of time). The greatest amount of time it would take to solve TSP (Big O notation, the measurement of time complexity, another concept that lies beyond the scope of this book) is exponential. Other NP problems include solving a Sudoku puzzle and scheduling students' classes while minimizing conflicts.

A problem that can be both solved and verified in polynomial time is classified as a **P problem**. Some common P problems in computer science are multiplying numbers, sorting data, and finding factors. Does it then follow that P and NP problems are not equal to each other? Maybe, but this question has not been proven either way, and if you can prove it, you will be the winner of one of the seven Millennium Prizes and one-million dollars richer!

Security

With all this sensitive and valuable data being transferred every second, it is important to keep it secure. You probably would not yell your social security or credit card numbers across a crowded room. Similarly, you should not send this data through insecure methods. There are several ways that malicious security **hackers**—"black hats" who exploit weaknesses on a computer or network—can steal or disrupt data. Some of these hackers just want to harm or break a network while others want to gather this data for other purposes, including identity theft or obtaining credit card numbers. Not all hackers seek to do harm. A hacker is any skilled user of technology who uses their prowess to solve problems. "White hat" security hackers explore the vulnerabilities on a computer or network—with the owner's consent—in order to help fix weaknesses and make data more secure.

In information security (InfoSec) there is a model designed to guide policies known as the **CIA triad** (not to be confused with the Central

Intelligence Agency). These letters stand for confidentiality, integrity, and availability. **Confidentiality** means that private data should remain private and companies should take steps to ensure that hackers do not access this information. **Integrity** means that data should be protected from being altered or deleted by hackers or non-human events. Finally, the **availability** of data means that all data should be accessible by authorized parties at appropriate times.

Malware is another name for malicious software. Hackers might carry out harmful tasks by installing such software with the intention of causing damage to a computer or network. Common types of malware include, but are not limited to, viruses, worms, logic bombs, Trojan horses, and botnets.

A **virus** is a program that infects other programs and usually spreads to other programs or computers by copying itself repeatedly. Most viruses spread due to user behavior. Opening an email attachment from an unknown source or plugging an infected USB drive into a computer can cause a virus to be installed. Once installed, it can be hard to remove a virus since it masks itself as another program. Luckily, today's anti-virus software can catch most of these threats. While viruses need an application to use as a host, **worms** are standalone pieces of malware that can disrupt a network. Like a virus, a worm spreads by copying itself repeatedly, but in the case of worms, human interaction is not necessary.

Viruses and worms often contain malicious code that will not execute until certain conditions are met. Such code is known as a **logic bomb**.

A common example is code that will delete or encrypt data after a fixed amount of time. A developer might also add a logic bomb to their code designed to trigger if they are ever fired from their job or after a set amount of time. In such cases, their former employer might have to pay them to fix this new "unknown" problem.

Malware can also be designed to hide its true intent. An app, advertisement, email, or game may seem innocent but, once opened or installed, deliver a malicious payload. In the Iliad, Homer tells of ancient Greek soldiers pulling a similar stunt at the gates of Troy by hiding inside a giant wooden horse, presented as a gift. This gift appeared innocent, but the payload was malicious. This type of malware is therefore known as a **Trojan horse**. Many Trojan horses serve as a **backdoor** to the infected computer, providing attackers with a way to access a device or network without permission. Not all backdoors are malicious, however. A company may need to access its employees' devices to provide technical support and security updates, for example.

Another way hackers cause havoc for a website is the **distributed denial-of-service attack (DDoS)**. In this method, hackers flood a site with fake requests, making the site's resources unavailable for legitimate users. This method does not steal any information or try to install any viruses, it simply hurts the site's business. Most websites can handle a lot of traffic, so hackers need to use huge numbers of computers for these attacks, more than a group of bad actors' computers can handle. Instead of trying to carry out this attack manually, they deploy a large network of Internet robots (bots for short), known as a **botnet**. To build a botnet, hackers distribute malware to a user's computer (or smartphone, smart TV, router, or other connected device), usually in the form of a Trojan horse. This Trojan horse's payload is a malicious **bot**. Once installed, the bot connects to a central computer called the command-and-control server that instructs the bot what to do next. These botnets are commonly used for DDoS attacks, but they can also be used for other malicious activities like spying and brute-force attacks, among others. There are many possible motives for a DDoS attack including spite, revenge, and blackmail. Defenses against DDoS attacks include blocking certain IP addresses and firewalls.

Hackers also try to steal data through **phishing**—using "bait" to trick users into entering sensitive information like usernames, passwords, or credit card numbers. Hackers may create a fake site or email that looks identical to a trustworthy website and try to get users to log in or update their information. Instead of logging in to the real site, though, this information is sent directly to the hackers, who can easily test these usernames and passwords on hundreds of other sites in a matter of seconds. **Spear phishing** targets a specific person or group using pre-existing knowledge. If phishing is trawling with a wide net then spear phishing is going after one particular fish. One way users can protect themselves against phishing is by always making sure the URL is correct before entering sensitive information. Any site can add a subdomain to the beginning of their URL, so https://amazon.com and http://amazon.ft543ffj.com are completely different domains (the

actual site is ft543ffj.com—more about domains in the next unit).
Another way that users can protect themselves is by making sure they
never use the same password for more than one website.

Password strength is equally important. Many users think if they use
a number and a symbol in their password then it will be hard to crack.
This is not the case. The main way to increase the strength of a
password is by making it longer. Hackers compile a list of passwords
they find every time data is data stolen. If a user's password is on that
list, it takes no time at all to break into their accounts. Hackers can
even test all these passwords to see if there is an at sign (@) in place of
an A or a dollar sign ($) in place of an S, so these common
substitutions do not increase password strength. Since length is the
main indicator of a strong password, something like
"*Bhdiu3fbEieef$nei3rf*" would be great, but it is doubtful anyone
would—or could—memorize a password like that for every site they
visit. Password management sites—like *1Password.com*, *LastPass*, and
KeePass—can be used to generate and store these random passwords.
Another technique is to combine four or more random words into one
long word. If one of the words is obscure, that's even better, so a great
password that is easier to remember than random characters could be
"paperelephantchartreusecoconut." This is longer than the previous
example but much easier to remember. It's a good practice to use a
password like this one to log in to a password management site and to
have this site store different, long, and random sets of characters for all
other sites. This way, you only need to memorize one password. It

should go without saying that you should keep this password secret—and don't use the example from this book!

A user can do everything right when it comes to creating a secure and unique password, but that's not always enough. If a company fails to take proper precautions when storing passwords, it does not matter how strong an individual's password is. If a hacker gets access to a company's database that stores user credentials in plaintext then the hacker would have a list of human readable usernames and passwords. Yet another reason to never reuse passwords! For this reason, passwords should not be stored in plaintext. Instead, only hashed versions of passwords should be retained. **Hashing** is the process of running data through a function—such as MD5, SHA-256, or bcrypt—that takes data of various sizes and returns a fixed length value, the hash. These functions are considered **one-way functions** since they are easy to calculate but hard to undo. Regardless of passwords' original lengths and complexities, all hashed value will look similar. Companies that use hashed passwords never even need to know the original passwords. They simply store the hashed values. When a user attempts to log in, the attempted password is run through the same hash function used to store the password, and the two values are compared to each other.

Using SHA256, the password hashes of *"paperelephantchartreusecoconut"*, *"123!"*, and *"grn734hdf$$fgdh!gs"* would be:

"90CE9D24B12D0F33BBC3F920392A9AF0A7994A59543FE844132EE298C547C1DE"

"58CC480580F302B31AC8C42D470DF5C3CC7ABEC35D99098288A5A3AC3B56A449"

"6CAA73EFBC5E0B49C481D25A1D5F1E9E57EB63B30102977707CB9257B34C5255"

respectively. All three hashed passwords contain the same number of characters, and any change in the plaintext passwords would drastically change their hashed values. It is not advisable to use SHA256 or MD5 for hashing passwords, however, since hackers can quickly compute them. bcrypt is a safer choice when dealing with passwords.

Cybersecurity is a cat-and-mouse game where attackers are constantly finding new ways to circumvent new safeguards, including hashing. Besides brute force, hackers can thwart hashed passwords by using a kind of dictionary attack known as lookup or rainbow tables. These attacks are effective because a given password, say "123!", will always return the same hash. To protect against these attacks, passwords can be **salted** before they are hashed. A salt is a random set of characters added to the password, resulting is something like "123!*34567fdh !*gj4*". Now the hashed result will look completely different every time "123!" is used. With a long and random enough salt, lookup and rainbow tables are not useful for cracking passwords.

Multi-factor authentication (MFA) offers a way to protect against hackers who do phish or steal users' credentials. MFA combines two or more methods of authentication. When exactly two methods are implemented, MFA is more commonly known as **two-factor**

authentication (2FA). These methods can combine something the user *knows*, something the user *has*, and something the user *is*. Something the user knows includes a password, a social security number, security questions, or any other knowledge that only the user should know. Something the user has includes a phone, a physical ID card, a debit card, a physical authentication token such as Yubikey or RSA SecureID, or a software authentication token like Authy or Duo. Something a user is includes fingerprints, a face scan, an iris scan, voice recognition, or even DNA. Using an ATM provides a well-known example of 2FA. The user needs their debit card (something they have) and their PIN (personal identification number, something they know) in order to access their bank account. If a bad actor steals your debit card, they cannot take all your money since they do not know your PIN. Likewise, if MFA is enabled and a hacker has your username and password, they would not be able to access your account without an additional form of authentication. This other form might be a six-digit code that changes every thirty seconds on a keychain fob or a text message or call to your cell phone. Either way, the hacker will not have this information, adding another layer of security.

Encryption

The most basic form of cryptography—methods for sending data securely in the presence of an adversary—is **encryption**, which is simply taking text and converting it so that it is illegible. The reverse process—converting the illegible text back into legible text—is known as **decryption**. To be able to encrypt and decrypt data, a list of instructions is needed. A **cipher** is a pair of **algorithms**—the lists of instructions—that give details on how to encrypt and decrypt the data. There is also a shared secret—or **key**—that is needed to make the encryption harder to crack.

One famous cipher is the **Caesar cipher** or Caesar shift where each letter is shifted the same amount. So if the shift (or key) was set to 1, then "A" would become "B"; "R" would become "S"; "X" would become "Y"; and "Z"" would loop around to the beginning of the alphabet and become "A." If the shift was 10, it would move each letter 10 places ahead and "A" would become "K." To decrypt the message, simply shift the key backwards.

Example:

> **Key:** 14
>
> **Plain text:** Computer Science is fun
>
> **Encrypted text:** Qcadihsf Gqwsbqs wg tib

This is a very simple cipher to use, but patterns of letters make it simple to crack or decipher. Using computers, this cipher would be solved in a split second.

Another example of simple encryption is the **random substitution cipher**. In this cipher, a letter is mapped or swapped with another letter in the alphabet, so "A" could be mapped to "F"; "B" could be mapped to "Z"; "C" could be mapped to "A" and so on until all 26 letters were mapped to another letter.

Example:

ABCDEFGHIJKLMNOPQRSTUVWXYZ

Key: SGPFNEYQUJKRCDVMIZAXHWOLBT

Plain text: Computer Science is fun

Encrypted text: Pvcmhxnz Apundpn ua ehd

This seems much harder to crack than the Caesar cipher, but it also has patterns, which makes it easy to break. This can be done quickly by a computer, but it can also be done by hand by looking at reoccurring sets of letters and letter frequency. The letter "E" is the most common letter in the English language, so whatever letter shows up most in the encrypted text is probably mapped to "E." If the same three letters appear multiple times, this could be the word "the," solving three letters at once.

A more difficult cipher to crack is the **Vigenère cipher**, which has similarities to the Caesar cipher and dates to the 1460s. As with the Caesar cipher, the Vigenère cipher uses a key to set the amount of letters the message will shift, but in the Vigenère cipher, the key is much longer and not the same for every letter. If the key was a phrase like "applesaretasty" then the first 14 characters would shift according to what letter was in the key at that place. The first letter would shift by "A" or 0, the second and third by "P" or 15, and so on. The fifteenth letter would start back at the beginning of the key. This process would then repeat itself until the whole text is encrypted.

Even though this cipher is difficult to crack, patterns and letter frequencies can still be used to find the key. The only way to make it unbreakable would be to have a key that was longer than the text itself, removing any patterns that arise (one-time pads use this method).

> **Example (**assuming "_" is the 27th letter**):**
> **Key:** APPLESARETASTY
> **Plain text:** COMPUTER_SCIENCE_IS_FUN
> **Encrypted text:** CDBAYLEI_WVIWGAE_XH_QYF

A famous example of breaking ciphers and decrypting messages can be seen in the film *The Imitation Game*, which tells the true story of Alan Turing, an English mathematician—he would be called a computer scientist today—who helped crack the German **Enigma machine** during World War II, allowing the Allies to read encrypted German messages and shortening the war by several years. A YouTube search will turn up videos that show exactly how the machine worked and how it was eventually cracked.

When talking about encryption, it is common to refer to two people communicating with each other while another tries to listen in. Traditionally, these two people are named **Alice** and **Bob** while the eavesdropper is called **Eve** (get it?). To use any of the previously discussed cipher examples, a shared key is needed that no one else knows. This type of key is called a secret or **private key**. If Alice and Bob both know the private key and Eve does not then encryption and decryption are simple. Eve will not be able to read the message between Alice and Bob, even if she intercepts it. Without the private key, the message looks like jumbled characters. Since Alice and Bob each use the same key both to encrypt and decrypt the message, it is known as **symmetric key encryption**. This method works well to send secret messages, but the problem is obtaining the private key. What if Alice is in New York and Bob is in Tokyo? If they try to send the key to each other then Eve may be able to intercept it en route and decrypt any future messages.

Public key encryption is a system that allows Alice and Bob to publicly publish a key that everyone, including Eve, can see. One way to think about public keys is by considering padlocks. Encrypting a message using Bob's public key is like putting a padlock on the message that only Bob has the key to, so if Alice wants to send an encrypted message to Bob, she encrypts it using Bob's public key. Only Bob has the information needed to unlock the "padlock" and read the message. Since the encryption key is different than the decryption key, public key encryption is also known as **asymmetric key encryption**.

Public key encryption works by creating a problem that is computationally hard, like the traveling Salesman dilemma described at the beginning of this unit. A computer could crack the cipher, but it would take several super computers hundreds or even thousands of years (Unless and until quantum computers become widely available. These machines could theoretically make cracking current encryption algorithms trivially easy). Even though public key encryption is tough to break, it is very simple to use. A problem that is easy in one direction and difficult in the other is known as a **one-way function.** Another one-way function, which is used in public keys as well, is clock or **modular arithmetic.** Imagine that an analog clock was set to 12:00 then someone moved the hour hand to 3:00. It might appear that the hour hand was only moved ahead 3 hours, but it could have been moved ahead a full rotation plus 3 hours which is 15 hours or 2 full rotations plus 3 hours which is 27 hours. It could have been moved ahead an infinite number of rotations plus 3 hours. It is impossible to know. The only person who has this information is the person who moved the clock ahead. This problem is easy for the person moving the clock hand but impossible for anyone who does not know how many rotations were made. In a very broad way, this is how public key encryption works.

Two of the most commonly used public key encryption algorithms are **Diffie-Hellman** (named after Whitfield Diffie and Martin Hellman) and **RSA** (named after Ron Rivest, Adi Shamir, and Leonard Adleman). Diffie-Hellman was one of the first public key encryption protocols and dates to the mid-1970s. Diffie-Hellman is considered a key exchange algorithm, a way to swap the private keys needed for other encryption algorithms.

RSA followed Diffie-Hellman. In addition to asymmetric encryption, it also allows for **digital signatures**. The digital signature is an electronic signature that, by using a public key, can be verified to be authentic. Both these algorithms are integral to security today.

Another application of public key encryption can be seen when browsing the web. It is important to trust the website being visited and also to have a secure connection, so Eve cannot see—or alter—what is being communicated between the user and the site. This happens every time **https://** is used. The "s" stands for secure and indicates that the Diffie-Hellman key exchange, RSA, or other methods are being used to secure the connection through a **digital handshake**. This process is called **Transport Layer Security (TLS)**. Its predecessor was **Secure Sockets Layer (SSL)**. TLS is the newer protocol, but this process is still referred to as SSL, even though TLS is being used. SSL uses a public key by authenticating a **Digital Certificate**, a trusted third-party file that verifies that the site is controlled by the legitimate owner. The entity that stores, signs, and issues these digital certificates is known as a **certificate authority** or **CA**. When possible, always use SSL (https) to visit websites. *HTTPS Everywhere* is a free and open source browser plug-in released by the Electronic Frontier Foundation and the Tor Project that forces https over http whenever possible.

Summary

Some of the largest and most profitable enterprises to ever exist in human history are built on the foundation of big data. In order to keep all this information secure, cryptography and other security practices are indispensable. As this book goes to press, data security and privacy are front-page news and the subject of heated congressional hearings. Given the power and profits built on the control of this information, the debate over who owns data, how it should be protected, and what it can be used for is unlikely to be resolved anytime soon. A basic understanding of the underlying technology is essential not just for computer users but for citizens. Similarly, networks drive the modern economy. In the following unit, we'll discuss the networks that connect computers to each other, especially the network of networks that is foundational not just to computer science but to modern life: The Internet.

Important Vocabulary

- **Asymmetric Key Encryption** – a different key is used to encrypt and decrypt a message

- **Availability** – element of the CIA triad stating that data should be accessible by authorized parties at appropriate times

- **Backdoor** – a secret way to bypass traditional access to a device or network

- **Botnet** – a large network of internet-robots called bots controlled by a command-and-control server, often used for DDoS attacks

- **Caesar Cipher** – a shift cipher where each letter is shifted the same amount

- **Certificate authority (CA)** – the entity that stores, signs, and issues digital certificates

- **CIA Triad** – in information security (InfoSec), the model designed to guide policies: Confidentiality, Integrity, Availability

- **Cipher** – a pair of algorithms that give details on how to encrypt and decrypt the data

- **Computationally Hard** – a problem that takes too long even for a computer to find the exact solution

- **Confidentiality** – element of the CIA triad stating that private data should remain private

- **DDoS** – distributed denial-of-service attack, hackers flood a site with fake request making all the site's resources unavailable for legitimate users

- **Decryption** – the reverse process of encryption

- **Digital Certificate** – a trusted third-party file that verifies a site as legitimate

- **Digital Signature** – an electronic signature that, by using public key, can be verified authentic

- **Encryption** – taking text and converting it so it is illegible

- **Hacker** – anyone who uses their technological skills to solve problems. A malicious security hacker exploits weakness on a computer or network and can steal or disrupt data

- **Hashing** – the process of running data through a one-way function that takes data of varying sizes and returns a unique fixed length value

- **Heuristic Approach** – an approach that gives results that are "good enough" when an exact answer is not necessary

- **Integrity** – element of the CIA triad stating that data should not be altered or deleted by unauthorized methods

- **Key** – in cryptography, a shared secret to make encryption harder to crack

- **Logic Bomb** – code that has been placed into software that waits to run until specific conditions are met

- **Malware** – malicious software intended to cause damage to a computer or network

- **Modular Arithmetic** – using the remainder when dividing, also known as clock arithmetic

- **Multi-factor Authentication (MFA)** – using two or more methods for verifying a user

- **NP Problem** – nondeterministic polynomial time, a problem that can be verified, but not solved, in polynomial time

- **One-way Function** – a problem that is easy in one direction and difficult in the other

- **P Problem** – polynomial time, a problem that can both be solved and verified in polynomial time

- **Phishing** – using "bait" to trick a user into handing over sensitive information like usernames, passwords, or credit card numbers

- **Private Key** – a shared secret needed to decrypt a message

- **Public Key** – a system that allows a key to be publicly published

- **Salting** – adding a random set of characters to a password before it is hashed to protect against rainbow table attacks

- **Spear Phishing** – a type of phishing attack that targets a specific person or group using pre-existing knowledge

- **SSL** – Secure Sockets Layer, issues digital certificates for websites

- **Substitution Cipher** – a cipher where a letter is mapped or swapped with another letter in the alphabet

- **Symmetric Key Encryption** – the same key is used both to encrypt and decrypt a message

- **TLS** – Transport Layer Security, issues digital certificates for websites

- **Traveling Salesman Problem (TSP)** – an NP-hard problem that, when given distances between pairs of cities, seeks to map out the shortest route between many cities and return back to the original city

- **Trojan Horse** – malware disguised to hide its true intent

- **Two-factor Authentication (2FA)** – a subset of MFA where exactly two methods for verifying a user are implemented

- **Virus** – a program that infects other programs and usually spreads to other programs or computers by copying itself repeatedly

- **Worm** – a standalone piece of malware that can disrupt a network by copying itself repeatedly without human interaction

6 - The Internet

"The goal of the Web is to serve humanity. We build it now so that those who come to it later will be able to create things that we cannot ourselves imagine."

- Tim Berners-Lee

Introduction

On its own, a computer is a useful tool, but when connected to other computers, its potential increases exponentially. As consequential as the introduction of personal computers was, its impact on society was not as significant as the introduction of many other technologies, such as the telephone, radio, or the automobile. This changed with the rise of the Internet. Is there any aspect of modern life that has not been altered by the Internet?

A computer **network** is a group of computers that are connected so they can share resources using a data link—either a cable or wireless connection. Networks can vary in size from those serving large businesses with thousands of computers that are all sharing files to a school with twenty computers to a family with three computers all connecting to the same home media server. The **Internet** is a network of these smaller networks connected according to a specific set of rules that computers use to facilitate their communications with each other. These rules are called **protocols** and the one the Internet uses is aptly named **Internet Protocol** (**IP**), which works closely with Transmission Control Protocol (**TCP**) and User Datagram Protocol (**UDP**).

The Internet is not as new as it may seem. Its origins date to 1969 and an agency of the U.S. Department of Defense called the Advanced Research Projects Agency (**ARPA**), which added the word "Defense" to the beginning of its name in 1972 to become **DARPA**. This agency created a packet-switching network appropriately known as the Advanced Research Projects Agency Network, or **ARPANET**. ARPANET was the first network to use the TCP/IP protocols that make up the Internet Protocol Suite, which is still used today (but which did not become the standard until 1982). ARPANET broke data up into smaller, more manageable pieces called packets (or datagrams in unreliable protocols, such as UDP), which continue to be the basis for digital communication today. Even though it was decommissioned on February 28, 1990, ARPANET is still considered the foundation of today's Internet.

The Internet Protocol Suite (TCP/IP Model)

While the Internet uses several communication protocols, it is built on the foundation of TCP/IP. In the early 1970s, DARPA researchers Bob Kahn and Vint Cerf built on earlier protocols to invent the Transmission Control Protocol (TCP). While it has been updated over the decades, TCP, combined with Internet Protocol (IP), remains at the heart of the Internet suite still used today. Because ARPA/DARPA originally funded the development of this model, it is also known as the Department of Defense Model (DoD Model). There are newer models that share the same name, but this book uses "**Internet Protocol Suite**" to refer to this original model. The Internet Protocol Suite contains four abstract layers. Abstraction—one of this course's "computation thinking practices"—is an important concept in computer science. In this case, it means that each layer focuses on its own functions and does not need to know what the other layers are doing. These layers are the application layer, the transport layer, the Internet layer, and the link layer.

The Application Layer

The application layer is the top layer of the Internet Protocol Suite. This layer defines rules for different user application and works closely with the transport layer to determine whether the data needs to be reliable or not.

One service that operates at the application layer is the World Wide Web. While many people commonly refer to the **Web** as if it is the entire Internet, they are not the same thing. The Internet has many services, which each use separate protocols at the application layer. The Web is just one of them. Other important application layer services and protocols include email (Internet Message Access Protocol or **IMAP**, Post Office Protocol or **POP**, and Simple Mail Transfer Protocol or **SMTP**), the Domain Name System (**DNS**), Internet telephony (Voice over Internet Protocol or **VoIP**), and file transfer (**FTP** or **SFTP**). Numerous protocols exist at the application layer including The Onion Router (Tor), Bitcoin, BitTorrent, Secure

Shell (SSH), and Remote Desktop Protocol (RDP). These protocols, along with many others, each provide specific services.

Websites display on browsers using the Hypertext Transfer Protocol (**HTTP**) or Hypertext Transfer Protocol Secure (**HTTPS**), which provides an encrypted connection between the browser and website (using **SSL/TLS** or similar, as discussed in unit five). For this reason, website addresses always begin with *http://* or *https://*. Although, modern browsers sometimes hide this part of the address.

Hypertext Transfer Protocol takes its name from Hypertext Markup Language (**HTML**), the standard language for creating web pages. A markup language is a way to format text so it stands out—changing colors, fonts, alignment, etc. It is not a programming language. HTML uses tags that are between angle brackets (< and >) and is usually paired with **Cascading Style Sheets (CSS)** and **JavaScript**. We will return to HTML and CSS in unit seven and JavaScript in unit eight.

A website is made up of files stored on a computer, also called a **server**. A server could be a home computer, part of a large server farm, or anything in between. When a computer requests a specific file (like a website) or service from a server, it is known as the **client**. The Internet runs on this **client-server model**. A client sends a request to a server then the server sends the requested information back to the client. The client can request the server by using its unique IP address (IPv4 or IPv6). It would be very tedious to memorize every IP address of every webpage, so instead, domain names are used.

A **domain name** is simply a name given or linked to an IP address. These are the website names that are typed into the web browser, like *google.com* or *wordpress.org*. Google's IP address is 8.8.8.8 (not that hard to remember) and WordPress's is 74.200.243.254 (among others). Domain names are broken into the **top-level domain** (TLD) and subdomains (including the **second-level domain** (SLD). Top-level domains are the highest level in the DNS hierarchy. They are the letters which follow the last period in the domain name, including *.com*, *.org*, *.edu*, *.net*, *.co*, and *.eu*. There are over 1,500 TLDs, which include countries and generic top-level domains, some of which may be restricted for specific purposes. Domain name assignments are managed by the Internet Assigned Number Authority (**IANA**), a non-profit organization which is a department of the Internet Corporation for Assigned Names and Numbers (**ICANN**).

Besides the home page, most websites contain many other pages or files. These files and folders use a Uniform Resource Locator or **URL** to call or locate specific files from the domain. An example of a URL is *https://www.youtube.com/watch?v=dQw4w9WgXcQ*. The domain name of this file is *youtube.com*. When a domain name is used on its own, the URL will usually default to opening a file called *index.html* or *home.html*, so entering the domain name *https://apcompsciprinciples.com* into your browser's address bar will cause it to open the URL *https://apcompsciprinciples.com/index.html*. Any domain can also be preceded by a **subdomain**, which is any domain that is part of another domain, so pages like *https://videos.apcompsciprinciples.com*, *https://www.apcompsciprinciples.com,* and *https://mail.apcompsciprinciples.com* are all owned by *apcompsciprinciples.com.* Organizations usually use subdomains when they want to allocate unique names to distinct parts of the organization, such as *videos* and *mail* in the examples above. Every domain outside of the top-level domains are technically subdomains, so *apcompsciprinciples* is both a second-level domain (immediately to the left of the top-level domain) and a subdomain of *com.*

Other parts of the URL include the protocol (usually http or https), the path to the file requested, and occasionally a port number. Paths dig deeper into the folders that contain the document and follow the top-level domain using slashes (/). A port number sometimes follows the top-level domain, indicated by a colon. The default ports are 80 for http and 443 for https. These ports do not need to be specified as they are used automatically for these protocols.

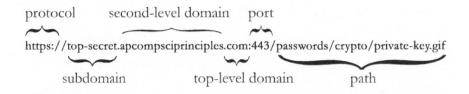

When a client requests a file from a server, the first thing the client needs to do is to determine the IP address of the URL's domain name, which is the function of the Domain Name System (**DNS**), a protocol on the application layer. The DNS is one of the smaller networks that make up the Internet and contains many servers that act like phone books. These computers are called **name servers** and contain many IP addresses and their matching domain names. The first step of retrieving an IP address is a DNS resolver. Many of these resolvers are owned by Internet Service Providers (**ISPs**), such as Comcast, AT&T, Time Warner, Verizon, Cox, and others. There are also other third parties who run resolvers, such as Google, Cloudflare, and OpenDNS.

Since there are so many IP addresses and domain names, the DSN is broken down into several steps. After the resolver check to see if the IP address is in its cache, it asks one of thirteen **Root Name Servers** that contain information about the appropriate TLD server to ask next. Most of the root name servers are networks of computers, providing redundancy in case of failure. They are named A–M and are maintained by a handful of different companies, groups, and universities. A few of these are Verisign, University of Maryland, U.S. Army Research Lab, and ICANN. The final step is to obtain info on the authoritative name server that contains the site's IP address.

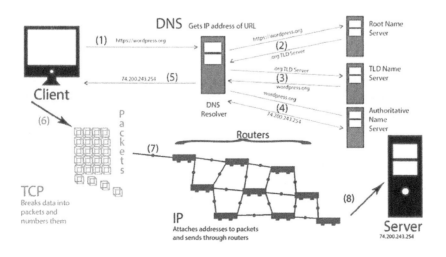

The Transport Layer

After a website's IP address has been obtained, the client's request can be prepared for transmission to the server by using transport layer protocols. The **Transmission Control Protocol** (TCP) breaks down the request into smaller, more manageable pieces called **packets**. TCP also numbers these packets, so when they are reassembled (on the server side), they will be in the correct order. When TCP finishes, the packets are handed off to the Internet Protocol found on the network layer of the Internet Protocol Suite.

The **User Datagram Protocol** (UDP) also breaks data down into packet-like structures known as **datagrams**. UDP works much like TCP but instead of numbering the packets, UDP sends the datagrams to the server without verifying whether any or all datagrams reached their destination. This protocol works best when time is of the essence, such as in video games or real-time audio and video. These applications cannot afford to re-request datagrams since the moment has already passed.

Since, TCP packets are numbered, it is easy to keep track of missing packets. If the server or host sees that packet number 25 is missing, it will request it again. Once the packet makes it to the destination, it is reassembled into the original file. This ensures that all packets eventually make it to the correct destination. Verifying that all packets are received increases the total time to send all packets, so there is a trade-off. That every packet will eventually arrive (or that their failure to arrive will be known) makes TCP reliable. A **reliable** protocol is one that lets the client know if all packets sent made it to the server. In contrast, when UDP drops packets, they are neither re-requested nor resent, so this protocol is generally faster but unreliable.

Overall, the Internet is **fault-tolerant**: Even if there is an error, the system will still work properly. Without this property, the whole system could fail if a single packet was misplaced, a cable was cut, or a router went down.

The Internet Layer

Once the data is ready to be transferred, the Internet Protocol (IP) creates addresses and attaches them to each packet, creating a way to keep track of packets as they travel across the physical Internet. Just as every business and home has a unique address so the post office can deliver mail, every computer and connected device has its own address, known as an Internet Protocol address or **IP address** for short. Even though everything on the computer is stored in binary, IP addresses are usually written in a form that humans can understand, like telephone numbers. Since every computer, printer, router, smartphone, and assorted device is connected to the Internet, the number of IP addresses in use is growing fast. Along with domain names, IP addresses are managed by IANA and ICANN.

Internet Protocol has gone through many versions, but the fourth version (IPv4) routes the most Internet traffic. IPv4 uses 32-bit addresses, which allow for a possible 2^{32} or 4,294,967,296 possible addresses. These addresses are broken down into 4 bytes, each separated by a period and displayed in decimal, giving a value from 0-255. An IPv4 address looks something like: **34.203.4.189**.

Four billion IP addresses seemed like more than enough back in the early 1980s when IPv4 was created, but with so many people on the Internet using multiple devices today, they have run out. In the late 1990s the Internet Engineering Task Force (**IETF**) came up with an addressing system that uses 128-bits, called IPv6. This allows for 2^{128} possible addresses, that is more than 3.4×10^{38} possibilities. This number is extremely large, much larger than the number of grains of sand or even the number of atoms on the planet. There will never be close to that many addresses. Since writing these addresses in bits require 128 ones and zeros, they are written in hexadecimal and might look like this: **2001:0db8:85a3:0000:0000:8a2e:0370:7334**. Since there are so many unused bytes, zeros can be omitted and replaced with a double colon: **2001:0db8:85a3::8a2e:0370:7334**. Most sites have both an IPv4 and IPv6 address to prepare for a smooth transition to using IPv6 exclusively, something that most people won't even notice when it happens.

Since IP addresses are stored in software, they can change and be deleted. For this reason, all devices that are connected to a network also have a unique, physical address stored in the computer's ROM. This address is called the media access control address, or **MAC address** for short. Since they are physically added by the manufacturer, a MAC address can also indicate what brand of device is attached to the address. In practice, though, malicious actors and others can easily mask or "spoof" MAC addresses.

The Link Layer

The link layer is the Internet Protocol Suite's lowest level. In the TCP/IP Model, this layer includes the protocols that manage the interface between physically connected nodes on a local network. The intricacies of the link layer are outside the scope of this course, but protocols included in this layer include the Address Resolution Protocol (ARP), the Reverse Address Resolution Protocol (RARP), and the Neighbor Discovery Protocol (NDP).

The Physical Internet

Unlike some Internet Protocol Models, TCP/IP does not specifically name a physical layer. Whether or not it's listed as a distinct layer, the next step in the process is physically transferring binary data from the client to the server.

Before any of this data can travel anywhere, it must first be converted (or modulated) from ones and zeros to the appropriate signal (light, electricity, or radio waves). A **modem** is the device that handles both the *mo*dulation, for outgoing signals, and the *dem*odulation, for incoming signals.

Once the other protocols have done their work, the data is sent to a networking device used to direct Internet traffic called a **router**. In home networks, routers are usually plugged into a modem, and it is common to see consumer products that serve as both router and modem. The newly made packets are sent to this router first. This personal router then sends the packets to the ISP's routers, and from here they are sent to many different routers along the "route" to the client. These packets are trying to find the fastest route possible using IP, so if there is high traffic at one router, they will take a different path. Much like roadways in the US, if there is a major accident or traffic jam, the cars (packets) will take a different road. The TCP's job of numbering and addressing the packets is important in case some packets don't make the trip. This is not uncommon. The client will simply ask for the missing packets by number instead of repeating the entire request. When the server receives these packets, it does the same process in reverse.

The server first collects the bits and turns them into packets then TCP arranges them in order and turns the packets back into a message. The request is then processed and sent back to the client in the same manner.

The closest part of the Internet's physical infrastructure, as mentioned above, is the first router that data is sent to. This router is usually a local business or home router. The data then gets sent to the ISP's router. For Internet provided over a cell signal (4G, 5G, LTE, etc.), the router is stored at the cell tower's location. Once the data reaches the ISP's initial point of contact, the packets are then sent through several more routers that are connected to the previous router by one of three mediums: electricity, light, or radio waves.

Electricity

One way to send these packets from one router to the next is by using copper wires. These copper wires send pulses that get converted to ones and zeros. Copper wire is found in most of the wires seen when connecting routers over a short distance and includes telephone wires (dial-up), DSL (another way to use telephone lines), Ethernet (cat5/6 cables), and cable Internet (coaxial). Category 5 and 6 cables are the predominant way to use electricity for networking today. Referred to simply as cat5 or cat6, these cables use twisted pairs (a method of twisting two wires together to reduce interference) to send signals over copper wires. There are a few potential downsides to using these cables. First, the signal can become degraded when sent over a long distance. Second, these wires are affected by electrical disturbances, such as lightning. Wired networking is usually much faster and more reliable than wireless, since there is less interference, but it is not nearly as fast as the speed of light.

Light

The fastest way to send packets, especially over long distances, is by using infrared light in the form of hair thin, transparent fibers called fiber optic cables (either single-mode or multimode). Not only is using fiber optic cables faster, but they also have a higher bandwidth and are not disturbed by electromagnetic interference. Fiber optic cables can consist of anywhere from a single pair up to several hundred pairs of fibers that can transmit light pulses that get converted back into ones and zeros by modems.

The two main types of fiber optic cable and are single-mode and multimode cables. **Multimode cables** are thicker (about 62.5 microns) than single-mode (about 10 microns) and can send light at different wavelengths through the same fiber. These extra wavelengths result in higher bandwidth but cause distortion over long distances (more than a few miles). For longer distances, **single-mode cable** is used. These are thinner and carry just one wavelength or mode but can carry a signal across very long distances.

While fiber optic cables are becoming more prevalent in large cities, they are most common in large underwater systems that connect continents. An interactive map of the cables resting at the bottom of oceans and where they connect to land can be seen on TeleGeography's website (https://www.submarinecablemap.com/). Once the data reaches land, it travels from router to router until it arrives at the correct location. Since this data is traveling at the speed of light, it takes a fraction of a second to travel from Europe to the United States. Most of the cable's girth is used to protect the hair-thin fibers that send the data thousands of miles in a split second.

Radio

The final way to transfer data is by radio waves. Radio waves are the part of the electromagnetic (EM) spectrum from 3 Hz to 3000 GHz. Since these waves exist on the EM spectrum, they travel at the speed of light—in theory. However the Earth is not a vacuum, so some mediums (gas, water, air, glass) slow the signal down while other things (cement, wood, humans) absorb some of the signal.

Some frequencies on the electromagnetic spectrum are used for AM and FM radio, broadcast television, satellite radio, microwaves, GPS, other forms of communication, and of course many Internet related transmissions. These frequencies are usually assigned by a branch of each country's government, especially since some frequencies do not travel very far. Lower frequencies travel farther since they face less electromagnetic interference and can better pass through objects. With so many towers available nowadays, high frequencies can be just as useful. US frequency allocations are public and are provided by the US Department of Commerce. Most television, cell phone, GPS, Wi-Fi, Bluetooth, walkie-talkie, and cordless phone signals are found in the UHF (ultra-high frequency) range, which spans 300 MHz to 3 GHz. Allocations are always changing as old technology becomes obsolete and new technology becomes more in-demand. The most popular wireless protocols have recently been rebranded as Wi-Fi 4 (802.11n), Wi-Fi 5 (802.11ac), and Wi-Fi 6 (802.11ax). Wi-Fi 4 works in both the 2.4 GHz and 5 GHz bands and can reach speeds up to 450 Mbps under perfect conditions. Wi-Fi 5 only uses the 5 GHz band and can reach speeds up to several Gbps. The newest Wi-Fi standard at the time of writing is Wi-Fi 6. This protocol debuted in late 2019 and can use all bands from 1 GHz up to 6 GHz, theoretically reaching speeds up to 11 Gbps under perfect conditions.

Most current cellular devices use a fourth-generation technology called 4G, and some are already moving to the fifth generation, aptly named 5G. 4G uses bands on the spectrum ranging, depending on the cell carrier, from 600MHz to 2.5 GHz. 4G brought speeds over ten times faster than 3G and paved the way for steaming video, ride-sharing apps, and more.

5G uses multiple bands of radio spectrum, but the most commonly discussed type is called millimeter-wave 5G. Millimeter-wave 5G uses frequencies from 24.25 GHz to 52.60 GHz and drastically improves not only bandwidth but also latency in comparison to 4G. Unfortunately, these speeds come at the cost of needing many more small cells to make up for the shorter distance that these radio waves can travel without degradation.

Speed

When sending digital data, everything is broken down to ones and zeros—or bits. The number of bits that can be processed per second is called the **bit rate**. The broader term **bandwidth** refers to the amount of resources available to transmit data and is usually measured in bit rate or frequency. **Latency** is sometimes defined as the amount of delay when sending digital data over a network but is more commonly understood as the round-trip time information takes to get from the client to the server and back. Latency is measured in milliseconds and can be found by pinging an IP address or URL. Since this data is traveling at the speed of light, latency between North America and Europe is less than 50 milliseconds, in other words, fast.

Summary

Since its origins as a communication tool for researchers, the Internet has grown to encompass nearly every aspect of modern life. Built on protocols—sets of rules—that allow computers on many different networks to communicate with each other, the Internet can seem like an amorphous, non-material thing: a cloud. But all this information is being sent through a physical infrastructure made up of modems, routers, and servers, each sending and receiving signals using electricity, light, and radio waves. While the Internet includes numerous protocols and is more than just the World Wide Web, for many, the Hypertext Transfer Protocol (HTTP)—the set of rules for transmitting websites—is synonymous with the Internet. In the following unit, we turn to the tools you need to create your own websites: HTML and CSS.

Important Vocabulary

- **ARPANET** – the Advanced Research Projects Agency Network, the first network to use TCP/IP

- **Bandwidth** – the amount of resources available to transmit data

- **Client** – any computer that requests a service

- **Cloud Computing** – using a remote server to store files

- **Datagrams** – Similar to packets, used in unreliable protocols such as UDP

- **DNS** – Domain Name System, one of the smaller networks that make up the Internet. It contains many servers that act like phone books

- **Domain Name** – a name given or linked to an IP address

- **Fault-tolerant** – a property of IP. If there is an error, it still works properly

- **FTP** – File Transfer Protocol, used for transferring files between a client and a server

- **HTML** – Hyper Text Markup Language, the standard markup language for creating web pages

- **HTTP** – Hyper Text Transfer Protocol, used for websites

- **HTTPS** – a secure version of HTTP that uses SSL/TLS

- **IMAP** – Internet Message Access Protocol, used for email

- **Internet** – a network of smaller networks connected using specific sets of rules that computers use to communicate with each other

- **Internet Protocol Suite** – Often referred to as TCP/IP, the four abstract layers in the DoD Model of the Internet

- **IP** – Internet protocol, a set of rules for sending packets over the Internet

- **IP Address** – a unique identifier for every device on the Internet

- **IPv4** – the version of IP that uses 32-bit addresses

- **IPv6** – the version of IP that uses 128-bit addresses

- **ISP** – Internet Service Provider

- **Latency** – the amount of delay when sending digital data over the Internet or the round-trip time information takes to get from the client to the server and back

- **MAC (media access control) Address** – a unique, physical address that is stored in the computer's ROM

- **Modem** – a device that handles both the modulation and the demodulation of signals

- **Name Server** – a server that contains many IP addresses and their matching domain names

- **Network** – a group of computers that are connected so they can share resources using a data link

- **Packets** – small chunks of data used in TCP/IP

- **POP** – Post Office Protocol, used for email

- **Protocol** – a specific set of rules

- **Reliable** – a protocol that lets the client know if the server received all sent packets

- **Root Name Server** – one of thirteen servers that contain every IP address and its matching domain name

- **Router** – a networking device that routes Internet traffic to the destination

- **Second-level Domain** – the second highest level in the DNS hierarchy, found directly to the left of the top-level domain in a domain name

- **Server** – any computer that provides a service

- **SMTP** – Simple Mail Transfer Protocol

- **Subdomain** – precedes the domain name, owned by the domain *https://subdomain.domain.com*

- **TCP** – Transmission Control Protocol, a set of rules for breaking down requests into smaller, more manageable, numbered packets

- **Top-level Domain** – the highest level in the DNS hierarchy, found to the right of the final period in a domain name

- **UDP** – User Datagram Protocol, like TCP and usually used for streaming media

- **URL** – Uniform Resource Locator, specifies where to find a file on a domain

- **VoIP** – Voice over Internet Protocol, used for telephony

- **Web (World Wide Web)** – the part of the Internet that uses HTTP and HTTPS

---

7 – Web Design: HTML and CSS

"A successful website does three things:

It attracts the right kinds of visitors.

Guides them to the main services or product you offer.

Collect Contact details for future ongoing relation."

- Mohamed Saad

Introduction

Since Tim Berners-Lee first deployed HTTP in 1989—more than thirty years ago—the World Wide Web has grown to a previously unimaginable scale, and websites have gained ever greater levels of complexity. There are now many useful tools available to craft complex and aesthetically pleasing websites, including HTML (Hypertext Markup Language) and CSS (Cascading Style Sheets) editors. A few popular pieces of software for writing and editing web pages are text editors (most are free or included with operating systems), Adobe Brackets (a free download), and Adobe Dreamweaver (not free). There are also free frameworks that can be used as a starting point, such as Bootstrap.

Editors

HTML and CSS can both be written with nothing more than a simple text editor. That said, countless tools exist to make the process easier.

Some of these tools are built into editors and include features like color coding, auto-complete, spell check, help finding bugs, and automatically closing things that need to be closed. A few popular editors include Notepad++, Sublime Text, TextPad, and Brackets. Some editors also support WYSIWYG (what you see is what you get), which is similar to changing fonts and colors on Microsoft Word.

HTML

Tim Berners-Lee created Hypertext Markup Language (HTML, currently in version 5.2) while working as a physicist at CERN. Berners-Lee is credited with creating HTML and the World Wide Web (not to be confused with the Internet) when he sent a March 1989 memo to CERN management titled *Information Management: A Proposal.* The original memo called this hypertext system "Mesh," but Berners-Lee renamed it "HTML" when writing the code in 1990.

As the name suggests, markup languages like HTML are similar to a draft term paper that an English teacher has marked up with a red pen. The markups are easily distinguished from the text itself. Instead of a red pen, HTML uses tags to add markup. These tags are contained inside *angle brackets* (< and >). Tags can be used to directly insert content (like images) into pages or can affect any text that is surrounded by an opening and a closing tag (such as paragraphs and links).

Basic Structure

The file extension *.html* indicates HTML files, but *.htm* extensions may also be seen. They're a holdover from the time when some systems could only use three-letter file extensions. HTML files all follow a similar structure:

```
<!DOCTYPE html>
<html>
    <head>
        <title>Title Goes Here</title>
    </head>
    <body>
    </body>
</html>
```

The first line defines the document type, which has become much simpler in HTML 5: *<!DOCTYPE html>*. The next tag, which surrounds the rest of the document, tells the document that anything between the opening *<html>* and closing *</html>* tags should be read as HTML. This tag is useful since things like CSS and JavaScript can also be embedded in an HTML file.

The next section is the header of the document, defined by the *<head>* and *</head>* tags. This section includes various metadata and the title of the page that will be displayed by a browser. The *<title>* and *</title>* tags are used to define the title.

The body of the webpage is the final part of the structure. Defined by **<body>** and **</body>**, it includes all visible elements of the page. Many other tags are used in this section. Here are some of the most common:

Heading	Six sizes of headings, h1 being the largest and most important: **<h1>...<h6>**
Paragraph	**<p>**
Anchor	used mainly for links: **<a>**
Image	**<img>**
Division	Defines sections of a webpage: **<div>**
Emphasis	Italicizes text and also emphasizes for screen readers: **<em>**
Strong	Bolds text and also affects screen readers: **<strong>**
Inline Frame	Used to embed other media into a webpage, such as YouTube videos: **<iframe>**
Comment	Used to add content that is not read by the web browser: **<!-- ... -->**

Attributes

Some tags contain attributes inside the opening tag's (or only tag's) angle brackets. Each tag has specific attributes that it can use. The site *https://www.w3schools.com* is a great resource for all available tags and attributes (as well as for CSS and JavaScript help). A few common attributes include *id, class, src,* and *href.* We will return to the *id* and *class* attributes in the CSS sections, but these attributes can be added to HTML tags as shown in these examples:

```
<p class="myClass" ></p>
<h1 id="uniqueID" ></h1>
<img id="pic1" class="leftImage" />
```

Notice that the name of the attribute is followed by an equals sign and the value assigned to it is inside quotes. Also, multiple attributes can be used by leaving a space between them. Other examples of attributes include:

```
<img src= "images/pic1.jpg" />
<a href= "https://somelink.com">My Link</a>
```

These examples define the source of an image to display and a hyperlink to reference, respectively.

CSS

Cascading Style Sheets (CSS) is a style sheet language used to describe the presentation—that is the look and formatting—of a document written in a markup language. The most common application is to style web pages written in HTML. CSS is designed primarily to enable the separation of document content (written in HTML or a similar markup language) from document presentation, including elements such as the colors, fonts, and layout. This separation can improve accessibility, provide more flexibility and control over presentation characteristics, enable multiple pages to share formatting, and reduce complexity and repetition in structural content, such as by allowing for table-less web design. CSS also allows the same markup page to be presented in different styles for different rendering methods, such as on screen or in print, on a specific device, or depending on screen width and resolution. While the author of a document typically links the document to a specific CSS style sheet, readers can use a different style sheet, perhaps one on their own computer, to override the one the author has specified.

CSS specifies a priority scheme to determine which style rules apply in case more than one rule applies to an element. In this so-called cascade, priorities or weights are calculated and assigned to rules, so the results are predictable.

To define CSS rules, an HTML file can either use the **<link>** tag to link to a separate file with the extension *.css* or use the **<style>** and **</style>** tags. When defining CSS rules, state the rule followed by braces ({ and }). Within the braces, all properties can be refined by listing the name of the property followed by a colon and the new desired effect. Each line inside the braces ends with a semicolon:

```
body{
    background: #fff;
    color: #545454;
    font-family: "Helvetica Neue", Helvetica, Arial, sans-serif;
    font-size: 16px;
    line-height: 1.5;
}
```

Rules

There are three general types of CSS rules: tag, class, and ID. The first type of rule is the **tag rule** which will redefine what an HTML tag looks like, including **body, h1, h2, h3, a, div, img,** and many more. The word tag here refers to the HTML tags in the document. There are over 90 available, but only a handful of them will be used often. A few of the most common ones are **body**, the heading tags (**h1-h6**), the anchor tag for links (**a**), **div** tags, the paragraph tag (**p**), and the image tag for pictures (**img**). As websites become more complex, more tags will be used.

```
img{
    float: left;
}
```

The **class rule** will be applied to any HTML tag belonging to a specific class. Their names always *begin with a period*. Class rules can be applied to any type and any number of HTML elements. They can even be added to small parts of elements like paragraphs or headings by automatically adding the <span> tags around the selection. Class tags can do countless other things, such as putting borders on tags, changing fonts or background colors, aligning elements, and adding padding or margins.

```
.standout{
    color: #222;
    font-weight: 600;
}
```

To add a rule to one specific element, **ID rules** are used. Since IDs are unique names for elements, each ID must be different. To create the rule for the ID, name it *beginning with the pound/hash symbol (#)*.

```
#didYouKnow{
    width: 400px;
    margin: 0 auto;
    padding: 2em 2em 4em;
}
```

There are also pseudo class selector rules, which include link:, visited:, :hover, and :active. They are usually preceded by the *a* tag (e.g. - a: visited) but can be used on any tag (e.g. - h2: hover). The cascading nature of CSS means that the rules at the bottom of the list happen last, so for links these rules should be created in the above order. If *hover* were to be listed above *visited* in the CSS, then hover would only work if the link had not been visited yet.

```
a:hover{
    text-decoration: underline;
}
```

Rules inside of rules can also be used, such as **div #container h1**. This rule would only be applied to an *h1* tag inside a *div* tag with the *ID* "container." If the same property needs to be added to multiple elements, they can be named and separated by commas:

```
div #container h1{
    color: #181818;
}

#container, h1, h2, .highlight{
    background-color: #b3b3b3;
}
```

Defining CSS Rules

So what kinds of things can these different CSS rules do?

Commonly used properties include margin and padding. These modify the box, which is an invisible border around all tags and is very useful when sizing and laying out a webpage. The box can easily be seen if a border or background is added to the rule.

By default, a tag's width is 100% of the page, and its height is only as tall as needed to fit the material. These proportions can be changed using width and height properties. *Float* determines what side of the page the tag is aligned to—left by default. *Padding* refers to the inside of the box and controls how close things are to the inside edge (think of a padded cell, which keeps the person inside away from the hard wall). *Margin* is the outside of the box and sets how close other tags can come to the edge.

@Media Queries

In addition to using CSS to change the look of the page, it can also be used to change the look of many other media queries. These queries include conditions that will check to see if the user is looking at a print preview, whether they are in landscape or portrait mode on a tablet or cell phone, and their screen resolution. There are many other conditions, including the most important one, max-width.

Max-width will check to see how wide the screen is and use the defined styles for this width. This is important when designing websites that respond to the device being used. Most websites should not look the same on a large desktop display as on a mobile phone. For example, little or no padding will be displayed on cell phones since real estate is scarce on such a small screen. Also, images may be different sizes on cell phone screens or even removed altogether.

To add these media queries, use @Media (min-width:1200px) {…}. The specific type of media would replace the content inside the parentheses, which is currently set for a minimum width of 1200 pixels. The rules for that media type would be inserted in-between the braces. This feature is useful when, for example, you need to define what a website looks like when displayed both in landscape mode *and* at a specific aspect ratio. Once the media query is added, add styles while the new media query is selected. The cascading property of CSS will make sure the new styles take effect since they are below the others on the style sheet.

When defining different styles based on width, a common set of break points are devices larger than 1200 pixels (large desktops), between 992 pixels and 1199 pixels (regular desktops and tablets in landscape mode), between 768 pixels and 991 pixels (most tablets in portrait mode), and smaller than 767 pixels (most smart phones).

```
@media (max-width: 600px){
    body{
        background-color: yellow;
    }
}
```

On a desktop, website content will move when the size of the window is changed. To avoid this, a container div tag (simply a div tag surrounding everything in the site with the ID: container) with a set width is used on the two largest screen sizes (e.g. width: 950px). Since tablet and smartphone screen sizes cannot be changed, it is appropriate to use percent of the screen when setting the width of a container div tag (e.g. width: 90%). It is also important to note that margins and padding will affect the percentage of a tag. This means that if a div tag is set to 100% and other elements around it have padding or margin, the width may be more than 100% of the page. To ensure that the page cannot scroll to the left or right, make sure that the total width of the elements does not add up to more than 100%.

Summary

With the skills introduced in this unit, you will be able to start creating your own websites that will adapt to whatever display they're viewed on, whether that is a giant desktop monitor or a tiny smartphone. HTML and CSS serve as the backbone of the World Wide Web, and you can write them using a simple text editor or with sophisticated, specialized programs like Dreamweaver. The original vision of the World Wide Web imagined a decentralized space where anyone could have their own website, linked to other websites through hyperlinks. With the rise of Facebook, Instagram, Twitter, and other social media sites, much creative expression on the Internet has moved into these corporate controlled "walled gardens," isolated from the wilds of the Web, but by creating our own websites outside of these corporate silos, we can help to maintain some of this original vision of the Web as a place where anyone can express themselves. The World Wide Web is undeniably important for contemporary culture and society, but at an even deeper level, code has come to define our modern economy. Familiarity with the basics of programming—the topic of unit eight—will provide you with important skills for navigating the modern economy.

8 - Programming: JavaScript

"To me programming is more than an important practical art. It is also a gigantic undertaking in the foundations of knowledge."

- Grace Hopper

Introduction

There are numerous programming languages in which software can be written. **Low-level languages** (binary, assembly, machine language, etc.) are considered "close to the metal" (that is the hardware) and have little or no abstraction. While these languages interface directly with the computer, which makes them run quickly, it is difficult for human beings to read or write them. **High-level languages** (C, Java, Python, etc.) are easier for humans to read, which makes them easier to debug. High-level languages also rely on abstraction and already existing libraries. A compiler or interpreter turns a high-level language into a low-level language before it gets sent to the hardware.

Since JavaScript cannot stand alone—it needs a web browser to run—many consider it a scripting language and not a true programming language, but JavaScript should still be considered a high-level language. First introduced in December 1995, JavaScript was originally developed by Brendan Eich of Netscape Communications Corporation. Along with HTML and CSS, JavaScript is one of the foundational technologies of the modern Web. JavaScript is a scripting language with a syntax loosely based on C. Like C, it has reserved keywords and no input or output constructs of its own. Where C relies on standard I/O libraries, a JavaScript engine relies on the host environment into which it is embedded, such as a web browser.

Debugging

Depending on the development environment, debugging can prove to be quite difficult. Since errors in JavaScript only appear in run-time (i.e., there is no way to check for errors without executing the code) and since JavaScript is interpreted by the web browser as the page is viewed, it may be difficult to track down an error's cause. Today's web browsers, however, come with reasonably good debuggers. With the arrival of integrated toolbars and plug-ins, an increasing amount of support for JavaScript debugging has become readily available.

For inexperienced programmers, scripting languages are especially susceptible to bugs. Because JavaScript is interpreted, loosely-typed, and has varying environments (host applications), implementations, and versions, programmers should take exceptional care to make sure the code executes as expected.

Errors

Programming can be a complex process, and errors can occur at any stage of development. There are several types of errors that can happen in programming, each with its own characteristics. One type of error is a **logic error**, which occurs when there is a mistake in the algorithm or program that causes it to behave incorrectly or unexpectedly. This type of error can be challenging to identify because the program may still run without crashing, even though the results are incorrect. One example of a logic error is adding when the programmer meant subtract, even the best debugger couldn't assume the intended intention.

Another type of error is a **syntax error**, which occurs when the rules of the programming language are not followed. Syntax errors are usually easier to identify because they typically result in the program not being able to run at all. A few examples of a syntax error are casing keywords incorrectly, spelling variables incorrectly, or forgetting a symbol; like a semi-colon, parenthesis, or quotation mark.

A **run-time error** is a mistake in the program that occurs during the execution of the program. Programming languages define their own run-time errors, which can include things like division by zero or accessing an invalid memory location.

Overflow errors are a specific type of run-time error that occurs when a computer attempts to handle a number that is outside of the defined range of values. Many programming languages represent integers using a fixed number of bits, which limits the range of values that can be represented. This limitation can result in overflow or other errors. Many programming languages use the most significant bit of a number to represent a positive or negative. So, if a number gets too large it could unexpectedly switch from positive to negative.

Round-off errors are another type of error that can occur when working with real numbers in programming. Real numbers are represented as approximations in computer storage, which can lead to limitations in the range of values that can be represented and mathematical operations on those values. This can result in round-off errors and other inaccuracies in calculations. Overall, understanding the different types of errors that can occur in programming is essential for developers to create efficient and accurate programs.

Development Process

In computer programming, the process of creating and developing software should be both iterative and incremental. It should be **incremental** in that it is done in small chunks and **iterative** in that it continuously repeats these steps. The main steps in this process are **design – implement – test**. The **design phase** consists of brainstorming and prototyping and is the most creative step in the process. The **implement phase** is putting the design into code. Since the design is already set, this phase should be the least creative. The **test phase** is checking to see if the code runs properly and finding errors or debugging the program. Since this process is iterative, the design phase is repeated after the test phase, and the program is constantly updated and improved. This process takes place every time a new version of software is released.

JavaScript

To insert JavaScript into HTML, you must use the <SCRIPT> tag. To close this tag when the JavaScript is complete, use the </SCRIPT> tag. JavaScript should be placed somewhere within the body of the HTML code, depending upon when and where the programmer wants to display their JavaScript program.

As with HTML, the computer does not read white space in JavaScript. Most commands in JavaScript, therefore, need to end in a semicolon to tell the computer when one command ends and another begins. JavaScript also uses programming's three basic logic structures: sequence, selection, and iteration. **Sequence** is the structure that runs one line after another, in order, without skipping or repeating code. So, after line 1 comes line 2 and after line 1001 comes line 1002. **Selection** uses *if statements* to select certain values, and **iteration** means to repeat a process. In programming this is accomplished by using loops. We will discuss selection and iteration in more detail below.

Comments are used to let the programmer—and anyone who looks at their code—know exactly what is going on. The programmer can use comments to define variables more clearly and to specify what they are trying to accomplish in certain areas of the program. Comments are especially helpful when going back to older projects after not looking at them for an extended period or when collaborating with others.

Using Variables

Variables are a way to store information. They can store many kinds of data, including text and numbers. Before they can be used, variables must first be defined. JavaScript uses the keyword *var* to set up a new variable. The word following *var* is the name of the new variable. The programmer may name this variable anything they would like. The name they choose should be relevant to what is being stored. For example: if the programmer is storing a string of text that says "Hello, how are you doing today?" then the variable might be called *greeting*. If the variable is storing someone's last name it might be called *lastName*. Notice that *lastName* is one word: Variables cannot have spaces nor can they start with anything except a letter. Also notice that the letter l in *lastName* is lower case while the N is upper case. This is called "camel casing" because the first letter is lower case and every new word is upper case, somewhat resembling a camel's humps. This is one way to avoid spaces. Using underscores is another way: *last_name*.

This line of code creates a variable named "greeting" that has nothing stored to it yet:

```
var greeting;
```

The 'let' Keyword

In JavaScript, the 'let' keyword was introduced in the ECMAScript 6 (ES6) specification in 2015 as a new way to declare variables. It differs from the 'var' keyword in several ways. Firstly, 'let' variables are block-scoped, which means they are only accessible within the block they are declared in, unlike 'var' variables which have function-level scope. Secondly, 'let' variables are not hoisted to the top of their scope like 'var' variables are, so they cannot be accessed before they are declared. Finally, re-declaring a variable using 'let' within the same scope is not allowed, whereas it is allowed with 'var', although this can lead to unexpected behavior. Overall, the 'let' keyword provides more control and predictability when declaring variables in JavaScript. For all example in this unit, the 'var' keyword will be used.

Strings

One thing a variable can store is a string, which is another way of saying text. A string may contain any character on the keyboard (even the space bar counts as a character). A string can be identified because it is surrounded by quotation marks. To create a string, the programmer must use quotation marks. "Hello, how are you?" is an example of such a string. Any input that is received from a prompt is in string form, even numbers.

```
greeting = "Hello, how are you?";
```

This line of code assigns the string "Hello, how are you?" to the variable "greeting."

Both creating the variable and assigning the variable can be combined into one step:

```
var greeting = "Hello, how are you?";
```

Numbers

A number differs from a string in that a string cannot be multiplied, rounded, or have any other mathematical operation applied to it. Another important difference is that, unlike strings, numbers do not have quotation marks around them.

```
var myAge = 17;
```

This command creates a variable named *myAge* and assigns it the value 17.

Alerts

The programmer can send a message to the user before they access the webpage. In JavaScript, this is called an *alert*. An alert pops up in a dialog box on the webpage. To make this happen, use the alert command:

```
alert("This is an alert!");
```

Notice that the parentheses contain a string. They could also contain a number or a variable. Whatever is written in the parentheses will be displayed in the alert. The command must end in a semicolon to let the program know it is finished.

A variable can also be placed inside the parentheses. Remember that there are no quotation marks around a variable!

```
alert(greeting);
```

Prompts

Prompts are like alerts in that they pop up in a dialog box. The difference between prompts and alerts is that prompts ask the user for input. Since input is coming into the program, it needs to be stored somewhere. Recall that variables are used to store information and that all inputs are stored as strings. The *prompt("Enter input: ", "Default Text");* returns whatever the user enters into the prompt. To store this input, let's assign a variable to this prompt:

```
var userInput = prompt("Enter your input", "type here");
```

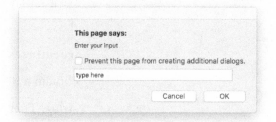

This command stores the user's input with the variable *userInput*.

Concatenation

To combine two stings together, *concatenation* must be used. Concatenation is the combination of two strings. To concatenate two strings in JavaScript, use the "+" sign. This operator can be used as many times as needed in the program:

```
alert("Hello " + username + "how are you?");
```

Converting Strings into Numbers

Remember that any input to the program is stored as a string, so whenever a user inputs something into a prompt, it is stored as a string. This is a problem if a number is entered into the prompt. For example, if 17 is entered into the prompt, it will be stored as "17", a string. In order to apply math to a string, it must first be converted into a number. The command to do this is ***parseInt( );*** and ***parseFloat( );*** for integers and decimals (i.e. floating-point numbers) respectively. Again, this command returns a number, which must be stored somewhere. The programmer probably does not need to keep the string "17" stored, so whatever variable was used to store it can be written over:

```
var userAge = prompt("What is your age?", "Enter age here");
userAge = parseInt(userAge);
```

The first line prompts the user to enter their age, which takes the form of a string. This string, which needs to be converted to a number, is inside the parentheses on the second line. The *userAge* on the left side of the second line is the new number.

Basic Math Operations

Now that there are numbers stored, mathematics can be applied to them. First, set up a new variable to store the solution then assign the equation to this variable. Addition (+), subtraction (-), multiplication (*), and division (/) can all be used here.

```
var dogAge = userAge * 7;
```

This line creates a new variable called *dogAge* and sets it to the user's age multiplied by 7.

Selection

Sometimes it is not necessary to run an entire script on a webpage. There are times when certain conditions need to be met to run a block of code. For example, if the user inputs their age, there could be a different alert for kids, teenagers, and adults.

If the user inputs an age below thirteen, they get one message. People between thirteen and seventeen get another message, and everyone eighteen and older gets another. This allows the computer to decide between multiple cases, called **selection** in computer programming. Selection, along with sequence and iteration are the three logic structures in programming.

If Statements

The way to provide separate selections depending on the user's age can be accomplished by using **if statements**. An *if statement* begins with the word "if" (notice the lower-case "i"). The condition that needs to be met follows inside the parentheses. Conditions use the following symbols:

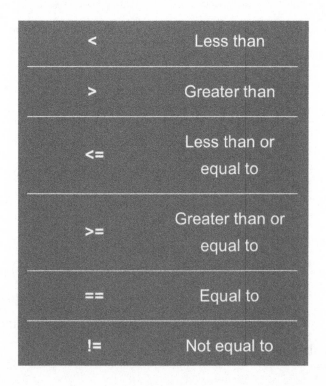

<	Less than
>	Greater than
<=	Less than or equal to
>=	Greater than or equal to
==	Equal to
!=	Not equal to

After the parentheses are closed around the conditional statement, braces { } are opened. *Notice: There is no semi-colon after the parentheses are closed!* If the conditional statement is true then anything that comes between these braces will be executed. If the conditional statement is not true, the code in the braces will be ignored.

A snippet of the code for the age program might look something like this:

```
if (age <= 12)
{
    alert("Enjoy your youth while it lasts!");
}
```

Else If Statements

If another *if statement* follows the first (usually conditions with the same variable), an **else if** can be used—this operator will connect the statements together. If the first *if statement* is true then the *else if statement* will be ignored. The order of the statements matters. These statements are exactly like *if statements* except for the word *else* before them.

This example might follow the snippet above:

```
else if ( age <= 17 )
{
    alert("Not too long before you can vote!");
}
```

Since the *if statement* above covers the ages twelve and below, this statement will only cover the ages from thirteen to seventeen. Why you ask? Well, if the age is twelve or below, the first *if statement* will be true, so the program will never get to the *else if statement*. There can be unlimited *else if statements* in the code.

Else Statements

The **else statement** can be used for any condition that is not met using the *if* or *else if statements*. The *else statement* works a little differently than the others because it does not need a conditional statement: It will only happen if the other statements are not true. In the age example, the *else statement* could look like this:

```
else
{
    alert("You are so old now!");
}
```

There can only be one *else statement* connected to each *if statement*, but the *else statement* is not necessary, nor is the *else if*. But there can never be an else if *or* else statement *without an* if statement!

Switch Statements

The **switch statement** is like the *if statement*, but rather than responding to conditions, the *switch statement* runs a segment of code for different cases. For example, the user might be asked to pick a number from a menu. The *switch statement* lets the programmer run different code depending on the user's input. The same thing could be accomplished with *if statements*, but it is much simpler with the *switch*.

The *switch* starts with the command:

```
switch(someVariable)
{
```

Notice: The block is opened with the open brace { (not a parenthesis)

someVariable is usually the variable that the user inputs. This variable can be anything from a single letter or number to a word or phrase. After the opening brace, the variable is compared to the available options and the appropriate code is run. In the *switch*, each option the programmer includes to be tested is called a *case*. To set up a case, simply write *case* followed by the desired input. If this desired input is a word or letter then it must be in quotation marks—unless you are using an existing variable. Numbers do not need quotation marks. A colon follows, which tells the computer that the code to run starts here. There can be as much or as little code as is needed. To tell the computer that the code is ending, the line **break;** is used. Without **break;**, the computer will not know the next case is beginning. Here are a few examples:

```
//Example 1:
case 1:
    alert("You have picked choice number 1!");
    alert("You can have as much code as needed here...");
break;

//Example 2:
case "yes":
    alert("You enter yes.");
    //all the code needed
    //even more code if necessary
break;
}
//when all cases are complete, make sure to close the
//switch statement with a close brace
```

If there is something that the programmer wants to happen if none of the cases are met then the *default* case should be used. Instead of the word *case* followed by a case, simply write the word *default* followed by a semicolon. Remember JavaScript is case sensitive.

```
default:
    alert("None of the cases were met!");
```

Notice that the default case is not followed by the line **break;**. Since this case must be the last one, it does not need to tell the computer that a new case is about to begin.

Iteration

Iteration means to repeat a process. In programming, it is accomplished by using loops. A **loop** is a block of code that the programmer wants to run more than once. The number of times a loop is run could be different in each situation. A loop might need to be run an exact number of times (e.g. ten, one-hundred, etc.), or a loop might need to be run until a certain condition is met (e.g. until a counter reaches a number or until the user picks the correct answer to a question). Two kinds of loops are *for loops* and *while loops*.

For Loops

For loops are the loops that are used to run a loop an exact number of times. *For loops* have three parts: The user must first initialize a counter variable. They must set a condition for the loop to keep executing, and they must set the increment by which the counter changes. The first part initializes a counter variable. The most common name for this variable is *i*. The next part is a condition that tells the loop how long to run: This condition would include the variable that was just initialized. It might look like this: $i < 10$. This means if *i* is less than ten, the loop will continue to execute. The final part of this loop is the increment, which tells how much to increase or decrease the counter variable. If the programmer wants to increase the loop by five every time it executes, then they would type: $i = i + 5$;. To decrease by twenty every time, the programmer would use: $i = i - 20$; and so on. Since increasing and decreasing the counter by one is so common, there is a shorthand way to write it: $i++$ and $i--$. These three steps are contained in one set of parentheses, and each of the steps is separated by semicolons.

The block of code that is to be run in every loop is contained in braces. Together, the entire loop looks like this:

```
for(var i = 1; i < 10; i++)
{
    Code to be run over and over goes here…
}
```

While Loops

A **while loop** is simpler than a *for loop*. *While loops* only have one part to them: the condition. For this reason, the programmer must set up a variable and make sure the condition is eventually met. An example of a *while loop* is prompting the user for a password. If the user guesses the incorrect password, the loop will continue to run, not letting user continue with the rest of the code.

```
var myPassword = "12345";
var userGuess = " ";
while( userGuess != myPassword)
{
    userGuess = prompt("Enter the password");
}
```

This code sets up two variables, one for the actual password and one for the user's guess. Notice that the user's guess is just set up as an empty string. The user has not guessed anything yet. The *while loop* has a condition that says, if the user's guess and the password are not equal, the loop will continue. Inside the loop is simply a prompt that asks the user to enter a password, so the program will continue to present the prompt to the user unless and until they enter the correct password.

Getting Stuck in Loops

The most common error with loops is using a condition that is always true. One case of this is if the programmer sets up a *for loop* that starts at one, whose condition is *i* < *10*, and decreases *i* by one every time. If *i* loses one every time then the condition of *i* < *10* will always be true. Therefore the loop will never end. If the computer gets stuck in a loop, two things might happen: (1) there might be an alert that never goes away, causing the user to exit the program, or (2) the computer tries repeatedly to carry out something that will never happen and tells the user that the program is not responding. Make sure the loops are not endless before executing a program!

Multiple Conditions

Inside things with conditions, like *if statements* and loops, the programmer might want to have a case where more than one condition needs to be met or at least one condition of many is met. Here the **&&** **(AND)** and **| |** **(OR)** symbols can be used. The **&** symbol is found above the 7 key (hold down the shift key) and the **|** symbol is found above the \ key (which is found between the backspace and enter keys). In a situation where a variable called *age* needs to be between 18 and 25 then the code could look like this:

```
if ( age >= 18 && age <= 25)
```

If the situation called for the age to be either younger than 18 or at least 55, this code would be used:

```
if (age < 18 || age >= 55)
```

Many of these connectors can be used in a single conditional statement, as in the following code:

```
while ( age == 18 && weight < 400 && height > 42 && hair == "blonde" && eyes == "blue")
```

Objects and Methods

JavaScript is an object-based programming language, which means that certain items in the language are stored as objects and that each of these objects has specific characteristics. Five important objects used in JavaScript are the **Math** object, the **document** object, the **string** object, the **Date** object, and the **array** object. Each of these objects has two features: *properties* and *methods*.

There are two different kinds of objects: objects that need to be set up by creating a new variable and those that can be used by simply saying the name of the object. The *new* keyword is used to create a new object to store in a variable, and this keyword needs to be used in the **date** and **array** objects. These objects will be discussed later in detail. The **string** object needs to be saved as a variable too, but the *new* keyword is not necessary. No variable needs to be set up for the **Math** and the **document** objects. Simply say *Math* or *document* when using these objects. Notice that *Math* is capitalized and *document* is all lowercase, JavaScript is CASE SENSITIVE.

Properties hold information about the object. In the *string* and the *array* objects, one property is *length*, which holds the length of the string or array. In the *Math* object *PI* is a property that holds the value of Π (approximately 3.14159). In the *document* object, some properties are *bgColor, fgColor*, and *title*. The *document* object deals with the webpage itself, so *bgColor* holds the background color, *fgColor* holds the foreground color, and the *title* is the title of the page. There are many other properties that can be found using a simple web search.

Methods are things the object can do. In the *Math* object, there are many methods, such as *sin, cos, tan, round, random, abs,* and *floor*. These methods *do* something to a number. They don't just hold information like properties do. In the string object, methods include *toUpperCase* and *toLowerCase*. These take a string and *do* something to them. They make them either into all uppercase or all lowercase letters.

In the document object, there are the *open, write,* and *close* methods. Here the *open* method *does* something by opening the HTML file so the file can be written to using the *write* method. After the programmer is done writing to the HTML document, it needs to be closed using the *close* method.

In the date object, the important methods are *getDay, getDate, getMonth, getHours, getMinutes,* and *getSeconds.* These methods retrieve information, in the form of a number, about the specified part of the date.

The array object, has many methods as well. Some of the common array methods include *join, sort, concat,* and *reverse.* These methods will be addressed deeper into this unit.

String Methods

Like numbers, strings may be manipulated in JavaScript. One common way to manipulate a string is to change it to all upper-case letters. To do this, we must call a method. Methods will be discussed in more detail later. To use this method, there must first be a string variable, which is just a variable with a string stored in it. *stringVar* will be the variable in this example. The period (.) is the way to call, or carry out, a method. Here the programmer would write the string variable, then a period, then the method. The output could be saved as another variable, or it could be placed directly into an alert. The method that is used to change strings to all CAPITAL LETTERS is **toUpperCase( )**.

Notice that this method does not have anything between the parentheses:

```
var stringVar = "this is my string";
alert(stringVar.toUpperCase());
```

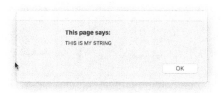

Similarly, there is a way to return the length of a string. **.length** is the method that returns the number of characters in a string. Recall that a character is anything inside the string, including numbers, letters, symbols, and even spaces. This method can be called the same way as **toUpperCase( )**, and the result can also be stored as a variable or placed directly into an alert. Here is an example that finds the length of a greeting:

```
var greeting = "hello, how are you?";
alert(greeting.length);
```

Here is a project that combines all the concepts learned thus far:

```
<script>
var greeting = "Hello";
var firstName = prompt("What is your first name?");
var lastName = prompt("What is your last name?");
var nameLength = firstName.length + lastName.length;
alert(greeting + " " + firstName.toUpperCase() + " " + lastName.toUpperCase());
alert("By the way, you have " + nameLength + " letters in your name");
</script>
```

Math Methods

To use one of the Math methods—or any method—the object must be called upon first. If the programmer wants to use the *round* method, first they would have to say *Math* (the object) then use a period to separate the object and the method. Together it looks like this:

$$\texttt{Math.round(3.1415);}$$

Here is a list of a few Math methods. More can be found in the appendix:

round(numVar);	Rounds to the nearest integer
ceil(numVar);	Rounds up to the nearest integer
floor(numVar);	Rounds down to the nearest integer
abs(numVar);	Returns the absolute value
sqrt(numVar);	Finds the square root of the number
pow(numVar, numVar);	Raises the 1st # to the 2nd #'s power
min(numVar, numVar, ...);	Returns the lowest of the numbers
max(numVar, numVar, ...);	Returns the highest of the numbers
random( );	Returns a random number between 0 and 1

Notice that the *random* method returns a number between 0 and 1. On its own, the usefulness of this method is extremely limited. A programmer is more likely to desire a random integer between, say, 1 and 10. To get this result, some math needs to be performed on the new number. First, multiply the random number by 10. Now it is a random number between 0 and 10—still not an integer. Next take the floor of the number—this makes the number an integer from 0 – 9. Finally, add 1 to the number to make it an integer between 1 and 10. These steps can be combined into one:

```
Math.floor( Math.random()*10 ) + 1;
```

Note that the order of operations does matter here. To change how many random numbers there can be, simply change the factor by which .random( ) is being multiplied. To change the first number, add the new starting number where the *1* is.

Date Object

The Date object is a little different than the Math object in that it cannot be used simply by saying the name of the object. Like the string object, this object should be stored in a variable. In the string object, the assignment operator was all that needed to be used. In the Date object, this is not the case. To assign a new instance of an object to a variable, use the keyword *new*. When setting up a new instance of an object, the *new* keyword precedes the name of the object, which is followed by a set of parentheses, usually empty. A line that causes all the Date object's information to be stored in a variable called *d* would look like this:

```
var d = new Date();
```

Now the programmer can use the methods associated with the Date object by placing the dot operator (a period) between the variable and the method:

```
var month = d.getMonth()
```

This line will store the number of the month in a variable called *month*. This number will take the somewhat awkward form of a number from 0 – 11, January being 0 and December being 11. A simple switch statement can fix this to display the correct month number or name. Similar steps also need to be taken for the day of the week and hour of the day.

An example of the code to make the date print out properly is on the following pages.

The Date Object - Displaying Date and Time

```
<script>
var date = new Date();
var dom = date.getDate();
var dow = date.getDay();
var month = date.getMonth();    //Create variables at
var year = date.getFullYear();  //the top of code
var mins = date.getMinutes();
var hour = date.getHours();
var amPm = "a.m.";

switch(dow)
{
    case 0: dow = "Sunday"; break;
    case 1: dow = "Monday"; break;
    case 2: dow = "Tuesday"; break;
    case 3: dow = "Wednesday"; break;
    case 4: dow = "Thursday"; break;
    case 5: dow = "Friday"; break;
    case 6: dow = "Saturday"; break;
}

switch(month)
{
    case 0: month = "January"; break;
    case 1: month = "February"; break;
    case 2: month = "March"; break;
    case 3: month = "April"; break;
    case 4: month = "May"; break;
    case 5: month = "June"; break;
    case 6: month = "July"; break;
    case 7: month = "August"; break;
    case 8: month = "September"; break;
    case 9: month = "October"; break;
    case 10: month = "November"; break;
    case 11: month = "December"; break;
}
```

```
if(hour >= 12)
{
    hour = hour -12;
    amPm = "p.m.";
}

if(hour == 0)
    hour = 12;

if(mins<10)
    mins = "0" + mins;

alert("Today is " + dow + ", " + month + " " +
dom + ", " + year + ". The time is " + hour + ":" + mins + " " + amPm);
</script>
```

Arrays

As programs become more complex, more variables are needed. An easy way to keep these variables neatly organized is with arrays. Programmers can create their own arrays and place whatever they want into them. Once an array is populated, more elements can be added without problems—unlike other languages.

The first step is to create the array, name it, and define how large it should be. The array itself is just another variable, so it looks like setting up any other variable. After naming the array, use brackets to define an empty array:

```
var arrayName = [];
```

Now that you have created an array with nothing in it, each element can be defined:

```
arrayName[0] = "something";
arrayName[1] = "stuff";
```

Remember that an array of size 2 has elements 0 and 1. In JavaScript, it is okay to add more elements than the size of the array as the array will automatically become one element larger. Another way to do the same thing is to add all the elements when the array is created.

Instead of leaving the brackets empty, put the array's desired content in the brackets:

```
var arrayName= ["something", "stuff",…];
```

Since arrays are objects, they contain properties and methods. An important property of arrays is **.length**. As with string objects, length returns the number of items in an object. The first index in an array is 0, so the last one is always one less than total number of elements in the array. This can be written as:

```
arrayName.length-1;
```

Knowing the length of an array is useful when an element needs to be added to the end of an array and the exact size is unknown or has changed. Since the last element in an array is length-1, the next element added would be at length. This can be written as:

```
arrayName[arrayName.length] = someValue;
```

length is also used when using a loop to run through every element in an array. A *for loop* starting at 0 and ending at the array's length-1 is best suited for an array. The following code will add *someValue* to every element in *arrayName*, regardless of the array's size.

```
for(var i = 0; i < arrayName.length; i++)
{
    arrayName[i] = someValue;
}
```

Arrays also have methods, which are useful in many situations. They can save time by eliminating the need to write code to perform these tasks. Examples include the **.sort( )** and **.reverse( )** methods. *Sort* arranges the elements in alphabetical order, and *reverse* flips the order of the elements in the array. These methods can be used together to first alphabetize the array and then flip it so the elements store in reverse alphabetical order, like this:

```
var newArray = arrayName.sort().reverse();
```

Other useful methods can be found in the *appendix*. They can do things like combine multiple arrays, add or subtract elements to the beginning or end of an array while shifting the position of the other elements, remove elements that have certain values, and so on.

Searches

An array can hold a large list of data, and it is useful to be able to search through the entire list to see if it contains certain values. Linear search and binary search are two popular search methods. A **linear search**, sometimes referred to as a sequential search, starts at the beginning and checks each element of the list one by one until it finds the item it is searching for. This algorithm is simple to write and is extremely fast if the list is small or the item is near the beginning of the list. If the list is long and the item is either not in the list or near the end, it can be "expensive," meaning it takes up a lot of memory. An advantage of linear search is that the list does not need to be in order.

A **binary search** works more like a game of higher or lower. By guessing the middle value of a possible range, a player can reduce the possibilities by half. Doing this repeatedly rapidly narrows down the possibilities, so guessing 50 when trying to figure out a number between 1 and 100 will eliminate half the range. If the solution is lower than 50 then 50 – 100 can be taken out of consideration. Guessing 25 next will cut the range in half again. A binary search works in the same way, so in order for it to function, the list must already be sorted. Because it doesn't have to check each item one by one, binary searches are usually less expensive than linear searches, especially with large data sets. Sorting the arrays first can be expensive, however, so there are tradeoffs between these two methods of searching.

Functions

There will be times when certain blocks of code might be used in different places in a program. Instead of rewriting this code multiple times, a function can be created. A function is like a method, except the programmer sets up exactly what happens when a function runs. The best place to put these functions is in the header of the HTML file. To create a function, simply write the word *function* followed by the name you want to give the function. Make sure the name is not already being used by any JavaScript methods or keywords. The name is followed by parentheses, which can be used to accept parameters. The function is then opened—like loops and if statements—with a brace. Inside the function there can be as much or as little code as necessary. The function ends with a return statement and a closing brace. The return statement is followed by whatever needs to be sent back to the place where the function was called. For functions that do not need to return anything, simply write the word **return;** followed by a semicolon, or leave it out altogether. The function will automatically return with no value when it hits the closing brace.

```
function nameTheFunc()
{
    //as much code as needed…
    return someValue;//optional if nothing is being returned
}
```

Now that the function has been created, it can be used whenever it's desired by using the line: **nameTheFunc( );** or whatever the programmer named it.

```
function myFunc()
{
    var firstName = "Bob";
    var lastName = "Smith";
    return firstName + lastName;
}
```

Like methods, functions can also take one or more parameters. Simply name the parameters in the parentheses and separate them by commas if needed. A local copy of this variable can then be used anywhere inside of the function.

```
function anotherFunc(firstName, lastName)
{
    var fullName = firstName + " " + lastName;
    return lastName;
}
```

Note: all the variables in this example are considered local and can only be used inside the function. If fullName is used outside this function then an error will occur—unless there is another local variable somewhere with the same name. This error can be avoided by using a global variable that can be seen by the entire code. To make a variable global, define it at the top of the JavaScript, above any functions.

```
var fullName;
function anotherFunc(firstName, lastName)
{
    fullName = firstName + " " + lastName;
    return lastName;
}
```

The only difference between these two examples is "var fullName" is defined as a variable before the function in the second example. Therefore "var fullName" does not need to be defined within the function. Because the variable fullName is global in this example, any function in the document can use and modify it.

Recursion

Recursion provides an alternative solution to an iterative problem. Any function that uses an iterative approach can also be written using a recursive function and vice versa. In programming, **recursion** is simply a function that references itself. A recursive function consists of two parts: a recursive call and a base call. The recursive call is the conditional statement that calls the current method again. The base call is similar to a condition in the iterative approach. It is the condition that, when met, causes recursive calls to stop being called and functions to start returning. As with the iterative approach, it is possible to get stuck in endless recursion, albeit resulting in a slightly different error. The code to find the factorial of a number illustrates how a function can be both iterative and recursive:

```
//recursive method
function factorialRecursive(var num)
{
    if(num > 1) //recursive call
        return num * factorial(n-1);
    else //base case
        return 1;
}

//iterative method
function factorialIterative(var num)
{
    var answer = 1;
    for(var i = num; i > 0; i--)
        answer *= I;
    return answer;
}
```

The Tower of Hanoi problem offers another popular example of recursion. In this problem, disks of decreasing size must be moved from one of three spots to another with the conditions that a larger disk may never be placed on top of a smaller one and that only one disk may be moved at a time. A quick Internet search will yield many interactive examples of this game. This game poses the kind of problem that recursion is well suited to since the solution involves unstacking a few disks then re-stacking them somewhere else many times, each time increasing the size of the new stack. When written out in code, Tower of Hanoi's recursive solution takes many fewer lines than the iterative solution, but the tradeoff is that—depending on the programming language—the recursive solution is slower due to the way in which functions are called.

A Google search for the word "recursion" will return a link at the top of the results that reads, "Did you mean: recursion," which links back to a Google search for "recursion." Hopefully it is clear why this little joke is (or is not) funny!

Events

Events are like messages or flags that objects can use to tell each other their state. The events discussed here are ones that tell when an action, such as clicking a button or moving the mouse over a picture, is performed by the user. Events are used as attributes of HTML tags, where they allow the programmer to run one line of JavaScript. There are many events, but the ones that will be most useful now are *onclick, onmouseover, onmouseout,* and *ondblclick*. The most common of these is the *onclick* event, which will run one line of code when added to a button (or picture—it works with any tag). This event is in the HTML code, not the JavaScript! In other words, the programmer must manually go into the code and find where the button is located. The easiest way to do this is by using the split view in the HTML editor. When the button is clicked, it should highlight the button's HTML code. Now, at the end of this opening tag (before the >) add the line **onclick = "yourFunction( )"**.

This event should still be inside the tag:

```
<input type = "button" …  onclick = "yourFunction()" >
```

If a button has been added previously then this tag already exists. There is no need to write it out again. The other three events work in much the same way. *ondblclick* will run the code if the button is double clicked. o*nmouseover* and *onmouseout* will run the code when the mouse hovers over the button and when the mouse leaves the button respectively. It is possible to have more than one event on a single button, such as *onmouseover* and *onmouseout*.

Event Listeners

Events work well in some situations, but the examples above use inline elements, which won't work well when applying or updating events to multiple elements or pages. Another drawback of events, inline or otherwise, is that only one of each type of event can be added to any given element. For example, multiple *onclick* events might not lead to the desired result, so for this reason, **event listeners** are more commonly used. Event listeners can be triggered by any HTML DOM event (such as *click, focus, keydown*, etc.) and can call a function (or anonymous function). They can define the way elements are ordered when the event occurs by using bubbling or capture, as well as other options, which are outside the scope of this unit.

The addEventListener() function is used to add an event listener to an element, such as a button. The parameters for this function are the DOM event, the function to be run when the event is triggered, and whether bubbling or capture are to be used (optional). The following example uses the first two parameters.

```
var myBtn = document.getElementById("btn");
myBtn.addEventListener("click", myFunc)
//myFunc() already defined
```

In this example and the one below, the event listener is added to an element with the ID of "btn". In the example above a function named myFunc will be called when the element is clicked. Notice this function does not (and cannot) use parameters. It is a reference to a function. The function is not yet being invoked or called. To use parameters, use an anonymous function:

```
var myBtn = document.getElementById("btn");
myBtn.addEventListener("click", function(){
//as much code to be run as needed
myOtherFunc(someParameter, anotherParameter);
})
```

Anonymous functions do not have a name and can include as much code as needed, including calling other functions that take parameters, unlike the first example. Arrow functions are shorthand syntax for defining functions that were introduced in ES6, as an alternative to anonymous functions, but fall outside the scope of this book.

Document Object

The document object, which is named *document*, is automatically loaded when the HTML file is opened in a browser. A useful method in the document object is **getElementById(str);** This method uses the *id* attribute of any HTML tags in the document. For example, if there were an image with the id: *myPicture*, it could be accessed using the following code:

```
document.getElementById("myPicture");
```

Element Objects

Element objects refer to the HTML elements within the document. Some elements are *body*, *h1*, *p*, and *input*. They are also called tags. These elements are typically referred to by their unique ID, as was seen above in the method **getElementById( )**. One important property of events is **innerHTML**. This property refers to the text in between the opening and closing tags of an element. In the HTML code: **<h1 id="myH1"> My Heading </h1>** the innerHTML is "My Heading." Depending on which side of the assignment operator this property is on, it can either read or write to the document.

```
document.getElementById("myH1").innerHTML =
"I Just Changed My Heading";
```

In this example, the *h1* would change from "My Heading" to "I Just Changed My Heading."

To save the current text in the *h1* tag with the *id* of *myH1* in a variable, the *innerHTML* would be on the right side of the assignment operator, as demonstrated in the following example:

```
var textInH1 = document.getElementById("myH1").innerHTML;
```

Note: If there is text already existing in the innerHTML—as in the first example—and a value is assigned to it then it will be replaced.

Forms

Another aspect of functions that makes them great tools is their ability to change hundreds of lines of code into just one. As we've seen above, when events are used, they can only trigger a single line of code. HTML employs forms when using items such as text boxes, text areas, check boxes, radio buttons, select (dropdown) boxes, buttons, and many other useful tools. JavaScript can be used to add some functionality to these things. With buttons, the most important thing is being able to tell the code that it has been pressed. This is one place where events come into play. Functions allow these events to trigger more complicated actions than a single line of code would be able to carry out.

Form Options

Besides buttons, other items—such as radio buttons, check boxes, select boxes, and text areas—can also go into forms. The programmer needs to make sure that these items are in the forms and that the forms are named with an ID. It would be simpler if there were only one form on any given page. To name a form, just add an *id* attribute to the tag remembering that JavaScript is case-sensitive. Most editors automatically give forms and form elements a default ID. Make sure to check the tag so that there are not two *id* attributes.

Without JavaScript, form elements do not have any functionality. Using JavaScript, these buttons, boxes, and text areas can be used to gather information from the webpage. Like forms, these items all need names, so the programmer can reference them later using their *id* attributes. Usually, these elements are automatically named upon insertion.

Once the forms and fields are all named with *id*s, functions can be created in JavaScript to add functionality. In most cases, something will happen if one of the *checkboxes* is checked. For example, if the user is purchasing something, the function might add to a total. For this type of function, an *if statement* could be used. First, tell the computer to look at the open document. Next, tell the computer what element is being evaluated by using **getElementById( )**. Now that the computer knows what it is looking at, ask the computer if this box is checked or not. If the box is checked, the computer will return true, and if the box is unchecked, the computer will return false. Such an *if statement* would look something like this:

```
if(document.getElementById("checkbox").checked)
{
        //do this if the box is checked…
        //.checked returns true of false so no need to
        //write == true
}
```

Radio buttons are like checkboxes except for one major difference: Radio buttons are all linked together. In other words, when one radio button is checked, no other button can be. To keep radio buttons connected, they are stored in an *array*. If five radio buttons are added, they will probably have names like R1[0], R1[1], R1[2], R1[3], and R1[4]. R1 is the name of the array. Each button is stored as an element in this array, starting at zero. To call on an element, square brackets are used [ ]. To show these radio button in an ID, they would be R1_0, R1_1, R1_2, R1_3, and R1_4. Even though there are five buttons, the highest element is four because they start at zero.

The *if statement* for a radio button looks like this:

```
if(document.getElementById("R1_0").checked)
{
    //do this if the box is checked…
}
```

Select (dropdown) boxes work like radio buttons in that the input they collect is saved in an array. The dropdown box itself is the array, and each option is an element. One attribute of select boxes is *selected*, which can be true or false. By using the method **.selectedIndex**, the index of the element that is currently selected will be returned (it will return *-1* if nothing is selected). The **.option** property can be used to call attributes of the individual options, but in most cases, simply using the **.value** property on the array is enough:

```
document.getElementById("select").value;
```

.value returns the selected element's value. Each element's value needs to be put in the array by adding an attribute or using the property pallet in an editor.

In cases where information needs to be retrieved or sent to a **text field**, simply assign a value to the text field or assign the text field to a new variable. Remember that whatever is on the left-hand side of the equals sign is being assigned a value. To save the content of the text field, type something along the lines of:

```
var stuff = document.getElementById("textfield").value;
```

To put something into the text area:

```
document.getElementById("textfield").value = "This will show up in the text area!";
```

With the skills introduced above, you'll be ready to start making websites that are more interactive than those made with HTML and CSS alone, but the principles of programming—including the development process, the use of variables, and iteration—will enable you to better grasp how computers "think" and to understand how software developers approach a problem.

Summary

In this unit we've had a chance to dig into the nitty-gritty of coding. Programming languages come in numerous flavors, including low-level languages that interface directly with hardware and high-level languages that are easier for humans to read, write, and debug. JavaScript is one such high-level language—one of the foundational technologies of the modern web—that you're now well on your way to mastering. While JavaScript is just one language with its own distinct syntax (loosely based on C), the basic principles of programming, introduced above, will serve you well no matter what languages you choose to learn in the future. In this unit, we've had a chance to spend some time with computers at their most technical. In the following unit, we'll take a step back and examine the social, economic, and cultural impacts of the computing revolution along with the ethical and legal quandaries posed by these impacts.

Important Vocabulary

- **AND** – basic logic gate where every part of a statement must be true for the entire statement to be true
- **Binary Search** – a searching algorithm, used on sorted lists, that divides the number of elements to search in half until it is down to one element
- **Constant** – used in coding to store a value that cannot be changed
- **Debugging** – finding errors in code

- **Design – Implement – Test** – the three steps of the iterative development process

- **Incremental** – done in small chunks

- **Iterative** – continuously repeating steps, achieved in programming by using loops

- **Linear Search** – sometimes referred to as a sequential search, a searching algorithm that starts at the first index and checks each element of the list one by one until it finds the item it is searching for

- **Logic Error** – a programming error that occurs when there is a mistake in the algorithm or program that causes it to behave incorrectly or unexpectedly

- **OR** – basic logic gate where any part of a statement can be true for the entire statement to be true

- **Overflow Error** – a specific type of run-time error that occurs when a computer attempts to handle a number that is outside of the defined range of values

- **Recursion** – a function that references itself and consists of two parts: a recursive call and a base call

- **Round-off Error** – a type of error that can occur when working with real that are represented as approximations in computer storage

- **Run-time Error** – a programming error that occurs during the execution of the program, like dividing by zero

- **Selection** – the logic structure in programming that uses *if statements* to select certain values

- **Sequence** – the structure that runs one line after another in order
- **Syntax Error** – a programming error which occurs when the rules of the programming language are not followed
- **Variable** – used in coding to store a value that can change

---

9 – Impact of Computing

"The Internet is not a luxury, it is a necessity."

- President Barack Obama

Introduction

Just a few decades ago, computers were oddities, operated by specialists and housed at universities, research facilities, and large corporations. With the introduction of the personal computer in the 1970s and 1980s, computing moved into homes, schools, and small businesses. During the 1990s the Internet became mainstream, connecting these computers—and their users—to each other. The first decade of the twenty-first century saw smartphones and other always-on devices make this digital connectivity nearly ubiquitous. While there has always been debate about computing's impact on society—note the Justice Department's 1990s investigation of Microsoft—it is only during the last decade that society as a whole has really started to grapple with computing's impact on society, both positive and negative. The mantra of Silicon Valley developers—that they're making the world a better place—began as a statement of optimistic faith in the power of technology before becoming a cliché and then a punchline. The beneficial effects of computing are impossible to deny, but it has become increasingly difficult to ignore the harms that offset the benefits of innovation. Additionally, computer networks have presented challenges to existing laws, such as those around intellectual property, privacy, and child protection. As computer users and programmers, we have an obligation to consider the impacts of our actions. We must ask ourselves whether our actions are ethical, not just legal, and we must learn about the steps we can take to protect ourselves and others, particularly those who cannot protect themselves, such as children.

Impact: Making the World a Better Place

Computers have provided exciting new tools for expressing creativity, solving problems, and enabling communication. Two decades into the twenty-first century, there is hardly an area of human activity that remains untouched by the power of digital computing.

In the photo editing and web design units of this books, we learned specific methods for using computers to showcase creativity. Many of today's most popular applications—from TikTok and Instagram to GarageBand and Canva—allow for the creation and sharing of images, videos, music, and more. There is little doubt that these easy-to-use and inexpensive (or free) tools have transformed popular culture.

As we saw in the compression, security, and programming units, computers can be used to find solutions to previously intractable issues. From deciding what song to listen to next to finding cures for diseases and sending humans into space, algorithms have become indispensable for solving problems both small and large.

The true power of computers only became apparent when they were networked together. One of computing's most significant impacts has been to enable communication and collaboration. Email, text messaging, and video conferencing have changed how we talk to each other. Services like Facebook and YouTube have transformed how we relate to our peers, families, celebrities, and politicians.

Digital communication enables new forms of collaboration. Git repositories like GitHub allow coders to work on programs simultaneously, while students can use tools like Google's G-Suite to coordinate class projects. Thanks to the Internet, such collaboration can take place among people who live thousands of miles from each other.

Computers also foster innovation and creativity by providing more opportunities for people to display and share their work more easily. Platforms and software like WordPress, YouTube, and Instagram allow artists and other creative workers to find audiences and engaged communities that may not have even existed before the rise of ubiquitous digital communication.

The benefits of easy communication, collaboration, and sharing can be seen clearly in free and open source software (FOSS). Open source projects can allow people to build on top of existing ideas, focusing on innovation without the constant need to reinvent the wheel. According to a 2012 estimate, if the FOSS operating system Debian—including the Linux Kernel, the GNU tools, and thousands of software packages—were to be developed from scratch, it would cost over nineteen-billion dollars. Other flavors of Linux, like Ubuntu, benefit from not having to redevelop all this software, as does the commercial operating system MacOS, which shares much of the underlying code. Projects like the Raspberry Pi, which includes an optimized variant of Debian, and much of the Internet, which runs disproportionately on Linux servers, would not exist without this spirit of collaboration.

Obstacles: The Digital Divide

Free and open source software reflects some of the most utopian possibilities of the computer revolution, but even here obstacles remain that prevent certain groups from fully participating. Indeed, a **digital divide** characterizes the computing field, holding people back along lines of gender, race, socioeconomic status, geography, disability or accessibility needs, and more.

One aspect of the digital divide has been access to the Internet itself. Funding for schools to provide on-campus access has been growing, but having access to the Internet at home seems to be an important indicator of academic success. Having broadband at home is directly related to socioeconomic status as well as geography since rural Internet access is often nonexistent, prohibitively expensive, or unusably slow. More affordable home Internet prices could help narrow this gap, but there are deep political divides as to how to achieve this goal, with proposed solutions including both decreased and increased regulation, public investment in infrastructure, municipal broadband, and cooperatives.

Online censorship falls along similar lines as the digital divide in internet access. Large online platforms have shown algorithmic racial bias when deciding when to leave or remove content that has been flagged as hateful. One study showed that white men receive more protection from hateful speech than women or people of color! In policing content, these platforms seem to deploy algorithms that negatively assess language more often used by minority groups.

The digital divide affects people with disabilities in terms of both access to information and greater online abuse. Laws exist that require websites and applications to provide certain accessibility options, so for example, a visually impaired person using a screen reader could still access the resource. Many disabilities, however, are not addressed by these tools, and compliance is far from universal. Online abuse can also discourage people with disabilities from using the Internet. More and better tools to prevent such abuse could improve the online experience for people with disabilities and other groups facing targeted harassment.

Computer science faces a massive and growing gender gap. Only a quarter of programming jobs are held by women. In 1984, 37 percent of computer science majors were women, but as of 2014 only 18 percent were. A 2019 study predicted that if current trends hold it would take one-hundred years for computer science researchers to achieve gender parity. This gender gap cannot be explained through any one cause. STEM-related toys have been marketed mainly to boys, and oftentimes boys have received more encouragement in developing an interest in technology (programs like Girls Who Code seek to close this early educational gap). And many women who seek to enter the field have been discouraged by an unwelcoming or even hostile climate, including outright discrimination and harassment. Whatever the cause, the gender gap has been economically damaging as necessary and lucrative jobs have gone unfilled. Moreover, engineers, like other people, inevitably work from their own perspectives, which has overwhelmingly meant male perspectives, leaving potential products undeveloped and potential markets unserved.

Lack of home broadband along socioeconomic and geographic lines, racial disparities in online censorship and protection against hateful conduct, lack of accessibility, and the preponderance of male software engineers are only a few aspects of the digital divide both in the United States and globally. Recognizing these obstacles to everyone's full and equal participation in the digital world is a first step toward ensuring that everyone can benefit from the positive impacts of computing. As long as entire groups of people remain underrepresented as creators and users of technology, the impact of technological innovation will not be able to reach its full potential.

Effects: It's Complicated

In the sections above, we've considered some of technology's positive impacts and the obstacles many face when trying to participate in the digital realm. Technology's impacts have not, however, been entirely beneficial. Technological innovation has had many effects on society, culture, and the economy, some of which have been harmful, intentionally or otherwise. Innovations that were created with the best intentions have had unintended consequences. Finding the balance and considering the tradeoffs between technology's beneficial and harmful effects can be tricky. Some recent or emerging technologies that present us with a mix of beneficial and harmful effects include social media, ride-sharing apps, and virtual reality.

Few technologies have impacted how we communicate in the twenty-first century more than social media, and there is little doubt that social media has brought many benefits. Sites like Facebook, Twitter, and Instagram have enabled people to make and maintain connections with many more people, even people who live thousands of miles away. These sites have also helped introverts connect with people in ways that feel more comfortable and have helped others to spread social awareness. On the other hand, research has found that heavy social media use can lead to anxiety, depression, and lower sleep quality. Social media can promote unhealthy comparisons with others, oftentimes leading to body image issues and cyberbullying. On a broader level, social media has been used to spread misinformation and outright lies, threatening democratic discourse and institutions throughout the world. Assessing whether the benefits are worth the cost is no easy task, and there is an enormous amount of evidence to stack up on either side. When making such assessments, though, it is important to remember that innovations cannot be considered in isolation. We need to weigh their impacts on society as a whole.

Just as social media has transformed how we communicate, ride-sharing apps seek to transform how we get around. These apps, however, have both positive and negative economic effects. Many drivers for companies such as Uber and Lyft like the flexibility that these apps allow. They can set their own hours and supplement income from other jobs, and more income means more spending, potentially benefitting their communities. On the other hand, if people choose to use ride-sharing apps rather than ride public transportation, we are likely to see increased automobile emissions and reduced government funding for transit, leaving those who rely on buses and trains as their sole means of transportation vulnerable. A full tallying of the benefits (e.g., reduced drunk driving, less need for individual car ownership) and harms (e.g. low wages, increased congestion, lack of accessibility) of ride-sharing apps is outside the scope of this book and is the subject of a vigorous public debate. As we develop our own perspectives, though, it is important to consider both sides with a fair mind.

Along with technology's social and economic effects, its cultural impact should not go unexamined. Virtual reality (VR) is an emerging technology that could have a tremendous cultural effect. People could have the opportunity to experience other cultures through simulations, broadening their horizons without the need to travel thousands of miles. They could learn the norms and traditions of other cultures without embarrassing mistakes and satisfy their curiosity without risk of offending real people. However, if VR becomes a replacement for rather than a supplement to real cultural exchange then people would lose the kind of immersive experience that enables a deeper understanding of other cultures. VR tourism could enable hyper-realistic "visits" to historical landmarks without experiencing the context of the countries where these landmarks are located. Many residents of hyper-touristed cities like Barcelona or Paris might welcome the reduced traffic, but others would lose the economic benefits of tourism. Either way, VR offers both the possibility of enabling cultural experiences that would not be possible otherwise and the threat of supplanting deeper real-world culture exchange that cannot be simulated.

Beyond these three examples, there are countless ways in which new technologies bring both positive and negative social, economic, and cultural impacts. Smartphones have put powerful computers and the potential of the entire Internet into our pockets but have also left us distracted, making it difficult to focus. Self-driving trucks might reduce highway crashes and increase efficiency while also putting millions of drivers out of work. Streaming video and inexpensive audio-visual equipment allows us to enjoy movies in the comfort of our own home but without the communal experience of sitting with others in a theater. When we develop new technologies—whether hardware or software—it is critical that we take a deep look into all the different ways these innovations can affect the world around us.

Intellectual Property

Let's say you've written the next hot app, recorded a song that you're sure is going to be a smash hit, or written the great American novel? What stops someone from coming along and copying your innovation? This issue is at least as old as the printing press, but digital technology makes it even more acute since one of the features of digital artifacts is that they are endlessly reproducible without any loss of quality. Governments have legislated a variety of solutions to this problem that are broadly grouped under the umbrella of intellectual property (IP). These are rights granted to authors and inventors for exclusive control of their creations, usually for a limited period of time. IP rights seek to promote innovation through the promise of financial gain, but when applied too broadly or for too long they can have the effect of stifling innovation by preventing the next generation of creators from building on the innovations of their predecessors. There is a long-running societal debate underway on appropriate levels of IP protections. What kinds of creations should receive what kinds of protection and how long should these protections last?

IP rights apply to intangible goods, so navigating them can sometimes be tricky. Following best practices and knowing existing laws can make it easier to protect your IP while respecting others'.

A patent is one form of intellectual property. **Patents** allow inventors to exclude others from using their inventions without permission and can last up to twenty years. Although patents have historically been applied to physical inventions, they can also be obtained for software. Legal and filing fees for a patent can run to several thousand dollars, and they can be difficult to defend in court.

Copyright is another form of intellectual property, which protects original forms of expression. In the United States, software is legally considered as a type of literary work for the purposes of copyright. In the U.S., copyright applies once a work is fixed in tangible form. It is not strictly necessary to register a work in order to receive copyright protections. However copyright registration provides for stronger protections under U.S. law and typically costs around $50. In the United States, copyright can last for the life of the author plus up to seventy years. The law does not prohibit "fair use" of a copyrighted work. Fair use allows certain exceptions to copyright for purposes such as education, news, and reviews, among others.

Trademarks protect brand names and logos in order to distinguish one company's product from other products on the market. Trademarks protect the source of a product rather than the product itself, so as nearly every soft drink manufacturer on the planet can tell you, there's no law against putting brown bubbly sugar water in a bottle or can and selling it. If you label your bottles as "Coca-Cola," however, you can expect to hear from a certain large corporation's lawyers very soon. It typically costs a few hundred dollars to register a trademark, which can last for a decade with the option to renew indefinitely.

IP can be a controversial topic. Mark Twain famously believed that copyright should last forever, like other forms of property, while others argue that high drug prices enabled by pharmaceutical patents lead to countless unnecessary deaths and so should not exist at all (Drug companies would respond that without the profits enabled by patents, these lifesaving pharmaceuticals would never be developed in the first place). Many others have staked out positions between these two extremes. With debates around IP law unlikely to be resolved anytime soon, developers and artists have worked together with lawyers to create licenses that promote cooperation and sharing. Two examples of such licenses can be found in free and open source software and Creative Commons.

Free and open source software allows you to use and build upon others' work and to allow others to use and build upon your work. The original free software license, the GNU General Public License (GPL), was written by Richard Stallman in 1989. It allows anyone to use, modify, or sell the licensed software for any purpose. The GPL is a "copyleft" license, which means that any new software built by modifying the original source code must also be licensed under the same terms. In this way, it uses copyright not to restrict access to IP but to promote cooperation. Some newer FOSS licenses, such as the BSD License and the Apache License are "permissive," that is they don't impose copyleft's share-alike conditions on derivative works. Whatever license is used, having access to the source code of free and open source software has security benefits since it is easier find—and fix—backdoors and other vulnerabilities.

Creative Commons is a non-profit organization founded in 2001 by IP lawyer Lawrence Lessig and others. It offers six main licenses that promote sharing of copyrighted works. Creative Commons licenses allow creators to permit others to use their work, subject to certain conditions, without the need to seek permission. Creative Commons licenses function much like open-source licenses and give creators an array of options that include allowing commercial or non-commercial use, permitting modifications of the work with or without the requirement to share-alike (imposing the same license on derivative works), and requiring or not requiring that attribution be given to the original author. In this way, Creative Commons allows creators to open up their work to be reused and remixed in a flexible and easy-to-understand manner.

Ethics

When designing software and using computers—as in other aspects of life—there are clear laws in place that prohibit certain actions. Using a computer to steal, spread malicious software, or plagiarize others' work is illegal, and breaking laws comes with consequences, including the possibility of criminal prosecution or civil penalties. However, the law provides, at best, a bare minimum standard of conduct. Just because something is illegal doesn't make it right.

Ethical computing demands that as users and developers we hold ourselves to a higher standard. Ethics refers to the principles, values, standards, and practices that guide individuals and groups in doing what is right. Bullying, using data for nefarious purposes, or gaining access to systems that you don't have authorization to access may or may not be illegal, depending on the circumstances, but these activities are probably not ethical. These examples are relatively clear but other ethical questions can be more muddled, and philosophers have argued since ancient times about which principles should guide moral values. Should we seek the greatest good for the greatest number, as utilitarians insist, or should we follow some version of the golden rule and do unto others as we would have them do unto us? These questions are not easy to resolve, but by weighing them we can develop our own personal and collective values. With this moral framework, we will have a better capacity to design innovations that take ethics into account.

Privacy and Security

The concepts of privacy and security are often confused, and they are often violated simultaneously, as during a data breach. While related, they are distinct concepts. **Privacy** deals with your personal information, how it is stored, and how it is shared. **Security**, on the other hand, refers to the steps companies take to protect your data. Protecting our privacy and security online often comes with tradeoffs, such as loss of convenience, but responsible computer users should not ignore these concerns.

How a company deals with personal data is usually spelled out in a lengthy end-user license agreement (**EULA**) that most people agree to without a second thought. Since EULAs are generally long, opaque, and purposely confusing, insisting on reading each of these legally binding agreements would make participating in online life virtually impossible. When you click "agree," however, you may be giving permission for a company to sell your data or to use it for its own profitable activities, such as targeted advertising, which may feel like a violation of your privacy. In other cases, your data might be sold without even this nominal form of consent, or it might be stolen in a data breach.

Even though many of these privacy violations are at least technically legal, there are several steps you can take to help safeguard your privacy online. These safeguards include taking action to limit sites from tracking you. One way to limit such tracking is by using a private browser that does not store cookies across sites. Another is by using a **virtual private network** (VPN) or related service to hide your IP address. On mobile devices, you can check your privacy settings to ensure that you have not given apps permission to collect unnecessary data, including location, contact information, or microphone and camera access. Both iOS and Android let you specify these permissions at the app level and ask that you accept them when the app is installed or first opened.

Deliberately long and confusing EULAs have done little to help consumers make informed choices about their personal data online. For many companies, protecting users' privacy is not a priority. Indeed, surveillance of user behavior has in many cases become central to their business models. As public opinion has begun to grapple with this reality, some laws have been passed to help protect personal data. The Children's Online Privacy Protection Act (COPPA), a U.S. federal law, protects children under the age of 13. The California Consumer Privacy Act (CCPA) applies to the largest state in the United States, where many tech companies are based, and the European Union's General Data Protection Regulation (GDPR) protects personal data both in and outside the world's largest single market. Each of these laws are unique, but they all aim to protect users and to provide more transparency into online companies' data collecting practices.

Corporate respect for user privacy is a necessary but not sufficient element of protecting personal data. If bad actors steal your private data then a company's best intentions are irrelevant. That's why security is also important. As discussed in Unit Five, hackers have many ways to access your data ranging from your mistakes (such as using weak passwords or falling for phishing schemes) to companies' failures to provide proper safeguards (such as storing sensitive data in plaintext). There are obvious things you can do to improve your security, including not reusing passwords, using multi-factor authentication where available, and learning to recognize phishing attempts. Unfortunately, you don't have much control over companies' practices. You can try to do business only with companies that have a solid track record of effective security, and you can hope companies follow existing laws and regulations intended to ensure that they safeguard personal data. As the number of high-profile data breaches increases, more companies are hiring Chief Information Security

Officers (CISOs) in order to avoid these embarrassing and sometimes costly mistakes.

Storing data in "the cloud," that is on distributed servers, raises its own questions in terms of privacy and security. Cloud computing is definitely convenient. It is easy to use, reliable, globally available, and cheaper to scale, but it is important to consider potential risks to privacy and security. There are trade-offs between cloud storage and keeping data on machines that you control. A few questions to think about when deciding whether to use cloud-based storage are who owns the data, can the service provider access the data, how often do they back up the data, what privacy and security measures do they have in place, can they use the data to advertise, and are you giving up privacy protections by putting your data into the cloud.

Whenever we make such decisions we face tradeoffs between privacy, security, convenience, and cost. Each person or group will feel comfortable with a different balance—and this balance will change depending on what kind of data we're dealing with. Many people will feel much more strongly about the privacy of their medical data or the security of their bank accounts than they will about a birthday message to their grandmother. Still, it is impossible to find the balance that is right for you if you're not informed about the available options and their tradeoffs.

Summary

Computers have become—for better or worse—an inescapable part of modern life. The benefits of the computing revolution are impossible to deny. Communication, sharing, and collaboration have been made easier and richer by the presence of computers in our life. Still, in many areas of life, the effects of computing have been murkier. The social, economic, and cultural effects of networked computers have been both positive and negative, and we would do well to keep these mixed effects in mind when evaluating new technologies. IP law both protects and sometimes stifles innovation, which has led to efforts to reform or add flexibility to copyright and other forms of intellectual property. Ethical computing demands that we, as users and developers, hold ourselves to a higher standard than what is simply legal, and as users and developers, we have an obligation to protect our own and others' security and privacy. In these areas, as in others, there are not always easy answers. Our decisions involve tradeoffs, but if we're informed and thoughtful about the impact of our actions, we can work to find a balance that we're comfortable with.

In the preceding nine units, we've had the opportunity to become acquainted with the foundations of computing and to learn a set of practical skills that will enable you to use computers more creatively and effectively. If you've made it this far, you have become a better informed and more skilled computer user, but you have also gained skills and knowledge that could make you a better artist, a more productive worker, and a more informed citizen. Computers have become central to modern society in a way that few imagined even a few decades ago. By mastering the principles of computer science, you are now better equipped to navigate the society we all share.

Important Vocabulary

- **Copyright** – a form of intellectual property, which protects original forms of expression

- **Digital Divide** – the gap between those who have access to technology and those who do not

- **Ethical Computing** – demands that users and developers hold themselves to a higher standard. Refers to the principles, values, standards, and practices that guide individuals and groups in doing what is right

- **EULA** – end-user license agreement

- **Patents** – allow inventors to exclude others from using their inventions without permission, can last up to twenty years

- **Privacy** – deals with your personal information, how it is stored, and how it is shared

- **Security** – refers to the steps companies take to protect your data

- **Trademarks** – protect brand names and logos in order to distinguish one company's product from other products on the market

- **VPN** – virtual private network

Suggested Reading

- Lawrence Lessig. *Free Culture: How Big Media Uses Technology and the Law to Lock Down Culture and Control Creativity.* New York: Penguin, 2004.

- Steven Levy. *Hackers: Heroes of the Computer Revolution.* Sebastopol, CA: O'Reilly Media, 2010.

- Safiya Umoja Noble. *Algorithms of Oppression: How Search Engines Reinforce Racism.* New York: NYU Press, 2018.

- Jenny Odell. *How to Do Nothing: Resisting the Attention Economy.* Brooklyn, NY: Melville House, 2019.

- Cathy O'Neil. *Weapons of Math Destruction.* Largo, MD: Crown Books, 2016.

- Eric S. Raymond. *The Cathedral and the Bazaar: Musings on Linux and Open Source by an Accidental Revolutionary.* Sebastopol, CA: O'Reilly Media, 1999.

- Astra Taylor. *The People's Platform: Taking Back Power and Culture in the Digital Age.* New York: Metropolitan Books, 2014.

- Siva Vaidhyanathan. *Intellectual Property: A Very Short Introduction.* Oxford: Oxford University Press, 2017.

- Shoshana Zuboff. *The Age of Surveillance Capitalism: The Fight for a Human Future at the New Frontier of Power.* New York: PublicAffairs, 2019.

Appendix - JavaScript Objects

String Object

var *yourVar* = "a string";

yourVar.METHOD( );

String Object Properties

Property	Description
length	Returns the number of **characters** in the string

String Object Methods

Method	Description
toUpperCase( )	Returns the string in all uppercase letters

toLowerCase( )	Returns the string in all lowercase letters
charAt(int)	Returns what character is at the specified index
substring(int1, int2)	Returns the string from index **int1** to index **int2 -1**
substring(int)	Returns the string from index **int** to the last character of the string
concat(str1, str2, ...)	Combines two or more stings together
sup( )	Changes the string into a superscript
sub( )	Changes the string into a subscript

parseInt(str)	Changes the string into an integer
parseFloat(str)	Changes the string into a floating-point number (decimal)

Math Object

Math.METHOD( );

Math Object Properties

Property	Description
E	Returns Euler's constant (approx. 2.718)
LN2	Returns the natural logarithm of 2 (approx. 0.693)
LN10	Returns the natural logarithm of 10 (approx. 2.302)
LOG2E	Returns the base-2 logarithm of E (approx. 1.414)

LOG10E	Returns the base-10 logarithm of E (approx. 0.434)
PI	Returns PI (approx. 3.14159)
SQRT1_2	Returns the square root of 1/2 (approx. 0.707)
SQRT2	Returns the square root of 2 (approx. 1.414)

Math Object Methods

Method	Description
abs(num)	Returns the absolute value of a number

ceil(num)	Returns the value of a number rounded upwards to the nearest integer
floor(num)	Returns the value of a number rounded downwards to the nearest integer
round(num)	Rounds a number to the nearest integer
min(num1, num2, ...)	Returns the number with the lowest value of x and y
max(num1, num2, ...)	Returns the number with the highest value of x and y
sqrt(num)	Returns the square root of a number

pow(num, num)	Returns the value of x to the power of y
random( )	Returns a random number between 0 and 1 (excluding 1)
sin(num)	Returns the sine of a number
cos(num)	Returns the cosine of a number
tan(num)	Returns the tangent of an angle

Document & HTML Objects

document.METHOD( );

Document Object Properties

Property	Description
bgColor	Sets or returns the color of the background
fgColor	Sets or returns the color of the foreground
title	Returns the title of the current document
cookie	Sets or returns all cookies associated with the current document

domain	Returns the domain name for the current document
lastModified	Returns the date and time a document was last modified
referrer	Returns the URL of the document that loaded the current document
URL	Returns the URL of the current document

Document Object Methods

Method	Description
getElementById(*"id"*)	Returns the element of a specific HTML tag using specified ID

blur( )	Takes focus off the element
focus( )	Gives focus to the element
click( )	Simulates a mouse click on the element

Element Object Properties

innerHTML	Sets text in between the opening and closing of specific HTML tags
style	Sets or returns the value of the style attribute of an element
className	Sets or returns the value of the class attribute of an element

Date Object

var *yourObj* = new Date( );

var *newVar* = *yourObj.METHOD*( );

Date Methods

Method	Description
Date( )	Returns today's date and time
getDate( )	Returns the day of the month from a Date object (from 1-31)
getDay( )	Returns the day of the week from a Date object (from 0-6)
getMonth( )	Returns the month from a Date object (from 0-11)

getFullYear( )	Returns the year, as a four-digit number, from a Date object
getHours( )	Returns the hour of a Date object (from 0-23)
getMinutes( )	Returns the minutes of a Date object (from 0-59)
getSeconds( )	Returns the seconds of a Date object (from 0-59)
getMilliseconds( )	Returns the milliseconds of a Date object (from 0-999)
getTime( )	Returns the number of milliseconds since midnight Jan 1, 1970. Also, known as Internet Time.

Array Object

var *yourArray* = [ ];

yourArray[0] = *something*;

yourArray[1] = *somethingElse*;

...

yourArray.METHOD( );

Array Object Properties

Property	Description
length	Returns the number of elements in the array

Array Object Methods

Method	Description
concat(A_1, A_2,...)	Combines two or more arrays and returns an array

reverse( )	Reverses the order of the array and returns an array
join(str)	Changes the array into a string and separates them with the specified string and returns a string
sort( )	Rearranges the array in alphabetical or numerical order and returns an array
push( )	Adds new elements to the end of an array, and returns the new length
pop( )	Removes the last element of an array, and returns that element
shift( )	Removes the first element of an array, and returns that element

unshift( )	Adds new elements to the beginning of an array, and returns the new length
splice(num and/or str)	Adds/Removes elements from an array
slice(int1 , int2)	Selects a part of an array, and returns the new array from index int1 to index int2-1

Events

Place the event followed by an equal sign and a function inside of an HTML tag.

<SOMETAG ... anEvent = "yourFunction( )">

Event	Description
onclick	When the mouse is clicked
ondblclick	When the mouse is double clicked
onkeypress	When a key on the keyboard is pressed
onkeydown	When a key on the keyboard is pressed down

onkeyup	When a key on the keyboard is released
onload	When the page is loaded
onreset	When the refresh button is pressed
onresize	When the page is resized
onselect	When text on the page is selected
onsubmit	When the submit button is pressed
onunload	When the page is closed
onmouseover	When the mouse is over the element

onmouseout	When the mouse is taken off an element
onmouseup	When the mouse button is released
onmousedown	When the mouse button is pressed down
onmousemove	When the mouse moves
onerror	When an error occurs on the page

Important Vocabulary

Abstraction – reducing information and detail to facilitate focus on relevant concepts

Additive Color – a color model where no light is black and the combination of all light is white, like RGB

AND – basic logic gate where every part of a statement must be true for the entire statement to be true

Application – almost everything on the computer except saved files and the operating system, including word processors, photo editing software, web browsers, games, and music programs

ARPANET – the Advanced Research Projects Agency Network, first agency to use TCP/IP

ASCII – American Standard Code for Information Interchange

Asymmetric Key Encryption – a different key is used to encrypt and decrypt a message

Atomic Transaction – transaction where all components must be carried out before the transaction is considered complete such that all occur or none occur

Availability – element of the CIA triad stating that data should be accessible by authorized parties at appropriate times

Backdoor – a secret way to bypass traditional access to a device or network

Bandwidth – the amount of resources available to transmit the data

Big Data – sets of data that are larger than a consumer software application can handle

Binary – base 2, number system that uses 0, 1

Binary Search – a searching algorithm, used on sorted lists, that divides the number of elements to search in half until it is down to one element

Binary Tree – a data structure that can, at the most, have two nodes or "branches"

BIOS – Basic input/output system

Bit – each number in the binary system, 0 or 1

Bit Depth – refers to the amplitude of the analog wave and specifically to the number of bits used for each sample

Bit Rate – the number of bits that can be processed per second

Boolean Logic – a branch of algebra where variables can only have two values: true or false

Botnet – a large network of internet-robots called bots controlled by a command-and-control server, often used for DDoS attacks

Byte – 8 bits

Caesar Cipher – a shift cipher where each letter is shifted the same amount

Central Processing Unit (CPU) – carries out every command or process on the computer and can be thought of as the brain of the computer

Certificate Authority (CA) – the entity that stores, signs, and issues digital certificates

CIA Triad – in information security (InfoSec), the model designed to guide policies: Confidentiality, Integrity, Availability

Cipher – is a pair of algorithms that give details on how to encrypt and decrypt the data

Citizen Science – a type of scientific research that is conducted, in whole or in part, by distributed individuals who contribute relevant data to research using their own computing devices

Client – any computer that requests a service

Cloud Computing – a type of distributed computing that involves using a network of remote servers to store, manage, and process data

CMYK – color model used for printing. Stands for **c**yan, **m**agenta, **y**ellow, and black (**k**ey), where the number associated with each letter is the percentage of each color used

Codec – a computer program that en*co*des or *dec*odes

Computationally Hard – a problem that takes too long even for a computer to find the exact solution

Computer – an electronic device that processes data according to a set of instructions or commands, known as a program

Confidentiality – element of the CIA triad stating that private data should remain private

Consistency – in databases, refers to the fact that information from one table does not contradict itself in any other table throughout a database

Constant – used in coding to store a value that cannot be changed

Copyright – a form of intellectual property, which protects original forms of expression

Core – the central processing unit (CPU), the main memory, the motherboard, and the power supply

Crowdsourcing – tapping into the collective intelligence of a large group of people to achieve a specific goal or solve a problem

CSS – Cascading Style Sheets, redefines mark-up in HTML

Datagrams – Similar to packets, used in unreliable protocols such as UDP

DDoS – distributed denial-of-service attack, hackers flood a site with fake request making all the site's resources unavailable for legitimate users

Deadlock – when, in a database, two transactions are trying to lock the same row and neither can continue until the other is complete

Debugging – finding errors in code

Decimal – base 10, number system that used 0-9

Decryption – the reverse process of encryption

Design – Implement – Test – the three steps of the iterative development process

Dictionary – a key in metadata explaining the instructions to encode or decode compressed data

Digit – each number in the decimal system, 0-9

Digital Certificate – a trusted third-party file that verifies a site as legitimate

Digital Divide – the gap between those who have access to technology and those who do not

Digital Signature – an electronic signature that, by using public key, can be verified authentic

Discarding Data – a type of lossy compression that removes unneeded data with no way to get that data back

Distributed Computing – a model that involves using multiple devices to run a program

DNS – Domain Name System, one of the smaller networks that make up the Internet. It contains many servers that act like phone books

Domain Name – a name given or linked to an IP address

Encryption – taking text and converting it so it is illegible

Ethical Computing – demands that users and developers hold themselves to a higher standard. Refers to the principles, values, standards, and practices that guide individuals and groups in doing what is right

EULA – end-user license agreement

Fault-tolerance – the ability for a system to continue to run properly even if one piece fails

Fault-tolerant – a property of IP. If there is an error, it still works properly

Fixed-length Code – blocks of code that are always the same size

FTP – File Transfer Protocol, used for transferring files between a client and a server

Graphical User Interface (GUI) – an interface that uses images to represent a system's folders and files

Hacker – anyone who uses their technological skills to solve problems. A malicious security hacker exploits weaknesses on a computer or network and can steal or disrupt data

Hardware – the physical parts of the computer, including devices such as the monitor, keyboard, speakers, wires, chips, cables, plugs, disks, printers, and mice

Hashing – the process of running data through a one-way function that takes data of varying sizes and returns a unique fixed length value

Heuristic Approach – an approach that gives results that are "good enough" when an exact answer is not necessary

Hexadecimal – base 16, number system that uses 0-9 and a-f

HTML – Hyper Text Markup Language, the standard for creating web pages

HTTP – Hyper Text Transfer Protocol, used for websites

HTTPS – a secure version of HTTP that uses SSL/TLS

Huffman Tree – a prefix free binary tree that is the most efficient way to compress individual characters

Idempotency – when an operation results in the same end result no matter how many times it is performed

IMAP – Internet Message Access Protocol, used for e-mail

Incremental – done in small chunks

Input and Output (I/O) Devices – how the user interacts with the computer

Integrity – element of the CIA triad stating that data should not be altered or deleted by unauthorized methods

Interframe Compression – a video compression that re-uses redundant pixels from one frame to the next, also known as temporal compression

Internet – a network of smaller networks connected using a specific set of rules that computers use to communicate with each other

Internet Protocol Suite – Often referred to as TCP/IP, the four abstract layers in the DoD Model of the Internet

Intraframe Compression – a technique used by compressing each frame of a video, also known as spatial compression

IP – Internet protocol, a unique address for every device connected to the Internet

IP Address – a unique identifier for every device on the Internet

IPv4 – the version of IP that uses 32-bit addresses

IPv6 – the version of IP that uses 128-bit addresses

ISP – Internet Service Provider

Iterative – continuously repeating steps, achieved in programming by using loops

Key – in cryptography, a shared secret to make encryption harder to crack

Keys – a database column that holds a unique value that distinguishes each record from others

Latency – the amount of delay when sending digital data over the Internet or the round-trip time information takes to get from the client to the server and back

Linear Search – sometimes referred to as a sequential search, a searching algorithm that starts at the first index and checks each element of the list one by one until it finds the item it is searching for

Logic Bomb – code that has been placed into software that waits to run until specific conditions are met

Logic Error – a programming error that occurs when there is a mistake in the algorithm or program that causes it to behave incorrectly or unexpectedly

Lossless – data compression that does not lose data during compression

Lossy – data compression that loses data during compression

MAC (media access control) Address – a unique, physical address that is stored in the computer's ROM

Main Memory – memory that temporarily stores information while it is being sent to the CPU, also called RAM

Malware – malicious software intended to cause damage to a computer or network

Metadata – additional data about the main data, usually at the beginning of a file

Modem - a device that handles both the modulation and the demodulation of signals

Modular Arithmetic – using the remainder when dividing, also known as clock arithmetic

Motherboard (logic board) - the standardized printed circuit board that connects the CPU, main memory, and peripherals

Multi-factor Authentication (MFA) – using two or more methods for verifying a user

Name Server – a server that contains many IP addresses and their matching domain names

Network – a group of computers that are connected so they can share resources using a data link

Nonvolatile – does not need a power supply. Information is physically written to the device

NP Problem – nondeterministic polynomial time, a problem that can be verified, but not solved, in polynomial time

Nybble (or Nibble) – half of a byte, 4 bits

One-way Function - a problem that is easy in one direction and difficult in the other

Operating System – software that provides common services to other programs, manages hardware and software resources, and provides the visual representation of the computer

OR – basic logic gate where any part of a statement can be true for the entire statement to be true

Overflow Error – a specific type of run-time error that occurs when a computer attempts to handle a number that is outside of the defined range of values

P Problem – polynomial time, a problem that can both be solved and verified in polynomial time

Packets – small chunks of data used in TCP/IP

Parallel Computing – breaks a program into multiple smaller sequential computing operations, some of which are performed simultaneously

Patents – allow inventors to exclude others from using their inventions without permission, can last up to twenty years

Peripherals – the input and output (I/O) devices and the secondary memory

Phishing – using "bait" to trick the user into entering sensitive information like usernames, passwords, or credit card numbers

Pixel – short for picture element. The basic unit of color on a computer display

Pixelation – when individual pixels are too large and the image begins to look blocky

POP – Post Office Protocol, used for e-mail

POST – Power-on self-test

Power Supply – converts AC electricity to the lower voltage DC electricity that is needed to power the computer

Prefix-free Code – a specific type of variable-length code that does not use pauses

Privacy – deals with your personal information, how it is stored, and how it is shared

Private Key – a shared secret needed to decrypt a message

Protocol – a specific set of rules

Psychoacoustics – a sub-branch of psychophysics that deals specifically with sound

Psychophysics – a branch of psychology that focuses on the fact that the human eye or ear cannot perceive the loss of certain data

Public Key – a system that allows a key to be publicly published

Random Access Memory (RAM) – memory that can be retrieved or written to anywhere without having to go through all the previous memory

Raster – an image format that represent data in a grid of dots or pixels

Recursion – a function that references itself and consists of two parts: a recursive call and a base call

Redundancy – finding frequencies or patterns in code

Relational Database – a database that has multiple tables that are connected by the use of unique keys

Reliable – a protocol that lets the client know if the server received all sent packets

RGB – color model used for most monitors or screens. Stands for red, green, and blue, referring to the color of light

Rollback – returning back to the state of a database before the write-ahead log began

Root Name Server – one of thirteen servers that contain every IP address and its matching domain name

Round-off Error – a type of error that can occur when working with real that are represented as approximations in computer storage

Router – a networking device that routes Internet traffic to the destination

Run-length Encoding – looking for redundancy or patterns as runs in the code

Run-time Error – a programming error that occurs during the execution of the program, like dividing by zero

Salting – adding a random set of characters to a password before it is hashed to protect against rainbow table attacks

Sample Rate – how often an analog signal is used when converting to digital, usually measured in kHz

Secondary Memory – used for long term storage and is physically changed when files are saved or deleted

Second-level Domain – the second highest level in the DNS hierarchy, found directly to the left of the top-level domain in a domain name

Security – refers to the steps companies take to protect your data

Selection – the logic structure in programming that uses *if* statements to select certain values

Sequence – the structure that runs one line after another in order

Sequential Computing – a model in which operations are performed in order, one at a time

Sequential Memory – memory used to store back-up data on a tape

Server – any computer that provides a service

Simpson's Paradox – a phenomenon that can occur when multiple groups of data trend in one direction but when combined with other sets the, trend disappears or reverses

SMTP – Simple Mail Transfer Protocol

Software – includes the operating system and the applications. It is usually stored on a computer's hard drive and cannot physically be touched. At the lowest level, it is a series of ones and zeros

Spear Phishing – a type of phishing attack that targets a specific person or group using pre-existing knowledge

SSL – Secure Sockets Layer, issues digital certificates for websites

Structured Query Language (SQL) – the language used to manage, access, and manipulate relational databases

Subdomain – precedes the domain name, owned by the domain *https://subdomain.domain.com*

Substitution Cipher – a cipher where a letter is mapped or swapped with another letter in the alphabet

Subtractive Color – a color model where no light is white and the combination of all light is black, like CMYK.

Symmetric Key Encryption – the same key is used to encrypt and decrypt a message

Syntax Error – a programming error which occurs when the rules of the programming language are not followed

TCP – Transmission Control Protocol, a set of rules for breaking down requests into smaller, more manageable, numbered packets

Text-based Interface – an interface made up of purely text input from the user

TLS – Transport Layer Security, issues digital certificates for websites

Top-level Domain – the highest level in the DNS hierarchy, found to the right of the final period in a domain name

Trademarks – protect brand names and logos in order to distinguish one company's product from other products on the market

Traveling Salesman Problem (TSP) – an NP-hard problem that, when given distances between pairs of cities, seeks to map out the shortest route between many cities and return back to the original city

Trojan Horse – malware disguised to hide its true intent

Truth Table – a table made up of rows and columns of Boolean variables and resulting Boolean expressions

Two-factor Authentication (2FA) – a subset of MFA where exactly two methods for verifying a user are implemented

Two-phase Commit Protocol – a standardized way for databases to make sure all transactions are able to write without any inconsistencies before committing

UDP – User Datagram Protocol, like TCP and usually used for streaming audio/video

Uncompressed – all the information from an original file in the same format

URL – Uniform Resource Locator, specifies where to find a file on a domain

Variable – used in coding to store a value that can change

Variable-length Code – each data block can be a different length

Vector – an image format that represents data through a combination of points connected by lines and curves

Virtual Tables – temporary tables that are made up of parts of other tables that help in reducing redundant data

Virus – a program that infects other programs and usually spreads to other programs or computers by copying itself repeatedly

VoIP – Voice over Internet Protocol, used for telephony

Volatile – needs a power supply. Turning off the power deletes information

VPN – virtual private network

Web (World Wide Web) – the part of the Internet that uses HTTP and HTTPS

Worm – a standalone piece of malware that can disrupt a network by copying itself repeatedly without human interaction

Write-ahead Logging – a method for avoiding inconsistencies in which all transactions are written and saved to a log before they are applied to a database